Symbology 101:

Everyday Letters, Decode the Vibrations

TheCosmicDoc

ISBN 13: 9781099310911

For my father, M. Mustakeem; as well as a very dear friend, teacher, mentor, and multidimensional angelic earth connection, Mrs. Elsie Milla. With me, she and I saw my father at the lighted table crossroads. Thank you both for eternally believing and reminding me that the future needs this and more sacred knowledge through empowerment most.

See the path, Trace the future.

Table of Contents

Symbology & The Vibrational Future

Symbols make the world, the universe, and multiverses go round. Centuries in between have made symbology a spirit science deeply unfamiliar, rendering many unable to decipher a vital language of the universe. Vibrations are central in the present and future, offering deeper core meanings beyond everyday superficial understandings. Symbology is the study of symbols. Symbols, however, are more than mere objects, circles, shapes, abstract designs or ancient drawings. They comprise a language, albeit hidden in plain sight in the mind/midst of many, that informs on levels never really imagined. Education of the masses in the 21st century does not include a basic understanding of vibrations and energy in everyday practice. However, the future is and will be based most on the reactivation of truth and the ability to see and read everyday letters of the English alphabet as a part of symbology and everyday knowledge.

The letters in your name, the numbers in your birthday, they all represent separate symbols influencing your ongoing vibrational life. Words, thoughts, letters, and numbers all project distinct yet varied meanings. These vibrational symbols not only make up who you and each of us is but moreover, these symbols transcend all time and space. They do as a language that is/has been changed, upgraded, and altered to fit societal needs, tremendous ego, as well as to appease powerful elite satisfaction content on using language as power through omission, denial, and active silences on the symbolic meaning of the past. The current English alphabet comprised of 26 letters is nowhere near how letters looked nor were symbolically used centuries before, however the power of symbology always persists. As time evolves, desires for power, meaning, and transmission have likewise changed. Those gifted with deeper sight, the seers able to understand and thus know symbols for their deeper core ancient intellectual insights can and will explain present-day evolution, lending assistance to millennial collective empowerment.

The future is ever changing, circling and cycling back to a vibrational core and way of being that once was and will again be in the future. This means most the reemergence of a universal language connecting you, me, each person, the planet, the many dimensions and multi-verses together through the symbolic vibrations of letters and numbers that always reveals more.

Historically, the more bold and authoritative tried to silence, alter, and/or dare try to destroy the legacy and symbolism of this universal language of vibrations. Such desires took and yet still take different forms and unexpected methods to thwart deeper core understanding of language as a power easily shared through symbols and cosmic meaning. The future will have far greater control with decoding abilities by gaining introductory understandings of symbols, letters, words, and numbers as expressed through the universal vibrational language.

You, me, and we all are apart of this once envisioned far off future of more that is here and represented strongest through words, names, letters; written and/or thought. Telepathy (ie speaking through the mind) the vibrational activation of communication is equally as powerful as what is written or verbally spoken. Therein, to really master language is to know and deeply understand symbols for what they show in helping us to see in ourselves, others and the evolutionary way of being in the multiverses. You are the letters, you are also the numbers - both of which are active symbols ever present in your life that extends far beyond many realms and will do so until the vibration is no longer remembered among future generations and societies. For power at its core is greatest through activation, continual use and memory of what once was/is/may perhaps forever be. Every symbol and all symbols have unending vibrational power to be remembered. Left to the choice of memory or lack thereof, the future far less empowered when unremembered. Forgetting opens to a void most of all. A void, comprised of emptiness and an overall long slumber that destabilizes and greatly erodes a future of profound cosmic knowingness.

May you learn, activate, and therefore symbolically know!

Symbols & Me

My symbolic connection of deeper understanding to universal thought is anchored within the very day I was born. According to one ancient mystic system, symbolically it shows that my entire life will always lead to seeking/thus revealing of hidden secret truths within the realms of universe/universal knowingness. The first letter of my born name being an S, vibrationally it means the rise of ancient wisdom, an unpredictable path of transformation and changes in life as well as being a transmitter, empowerer, and lightbringer of sacred knowledge that is past life connected with potential to expand the future in a myriad of unexpected yet dynamically mystical ways.

More than that, I was raised at a very young age to focus and see patterns quickly through countless additional math and writing homework assignments my mother required, on any and virtually every day including weekends. Along with that she and I would play memory card games with an ordinary deck of playing cards which years later my mother explained was to increase my focus, concentration, memory, and to further develop my ability to see patterns at a rapid pace. Both of my parents in fact harnessed the ability of discernment allowing me to better see symbological patterns quickly and universally much more. Additionally, being a Sun a Taurus coincides with the who and how relative to common tendencies of Tauruses to rely on evaluating patterns, behaviors and creating categories to make sense of the evolving world vibrationally by decoding it and the people in it.

Likewise, taking on the original name *TheCosmicDoc*, the letters decoded reveal that I came to empower through many doors of knowledge and deeper cosmic understandings. As a child I never felt unique in any particular way. However, I was born able to process information at quick and extremely high levels, had incredible focus almost unusual for a child, a relatively sharp memory, and the ability to see and remember patterns. While my life seemed "normal" to me, moving onward, as I remained staunch with my mom about my higher learning - through education both inside and outside of the classroom - it was in graduate school many years later that I began to double my learning by teaching myself the vibrational knowledge of symbols and symbology from a soul memory level. I did so largely through studying destiny cards and numbers. As I explain in my first cosmic book, *Numerology 101*, numbers are symbols, and symbols have long been central throughout my entire life. They are apart of the destined plan of my soul contract, much of which involves a high sensory psychic mediumship, cosmic decoding, and active channeling for a great many far beyond myself, my mind, and my own personal enrichment.

At this point in my life fully accepting the divine fact that I AM a seer able to vibrationally read with ancient knowing and remembrance enables the unlocking of many worldly things: letters, numbers, people, and multidimensional symbols. The cosmos speak to me most through symbols and frequencies that I can feel. I see the universal core of any name, word, number, and much more. I likewise am and have long been a dreamer able to see and interpret symbolism and messages of the future and higher realms within dreams. Symbols through my eyes emerge any/everywhere often on walls, people, floors, and even animals. While also being a Usui/Karuna Reiki Master female of color, a shamanic healer of many divine abilities and sight makes symbols activate and thus come alive in clear form for my vibrational awareness and immediate recognition. My born name means a wise healer, a seer of high sight on the direct path to God/multiverses. When I served as a local psychic medium and radio personality in St. Louis, MO as *TheCosmicDoc*, I gave live readings to callers through an original show I developed and was invited to offer weekly on air for over a year on 100.3 TheBeat called "Music and Predictions". Callers gave both their name and birthday which I used to read them based not only on my intuition as a high sensory empath and psychic medium, but also by examining the letters in each person's name which offered me precise understanding of them, their destined purposes, and a basic glimpse of their behavioral patterns.

We are all capable of seeing within the universe through divine sight. What follows, I offer as an open channel for you to expand your mind and vibrational understandings in direct connection to the language of the universe/multiverses/multi-dimensions and ultimately the cosmos and most of all to know you more. Your learning and symbolic knowingness are apart of the future, the prophecies, and most of all the active and rigorous desire to know more beyond the illusion of untruths and hidden knowledge.

Above all, may you learn thyself and how to actively decode the coming future.

Letters: Cosmic Symbols Hidden in Plain Sight

Letters are key and among the keys most critical to this vibrational future if and when they are seen, understood, and read as symbols. Both letters and numbers are living vibrations all around and for many still hidden in plain sight. To know is to understand. Letters once vibrationally seen/read and thus decoded become the wayshowers of and to the past, present, and future. Every letter, word, every paragraph, page, and thoughts are comprised of distinct vibrations combined through the letters and words contained within. Seeing letters as more than casual language, but signs of mystical and universal revelation can inform the present what the future will be seen as an everyday, expected, and common vibrational of knowingness emerging from centuries and cycles before once hidden, banned, defamed, re-theorized, rewritten, leading therefore to knowledge systems becoming forgotten and therefore unknown.

We live in a matrix of signs and symbols represented by letters and the numbers. There are currently 26 letters in the alphabet which as such facilitates enable the finding of one's power (8 vibration), using the mind and emotions (2 vibration), and becoming more conscientious in the body, mind, and spirit (6 vibration). Without basic decoding to understand the multiverses - (already well versed in active vibrational understanding and exchange), we may never know deeper universal/cosmic truths that lie in future wait. What is hidden is done so for, by, and with particular motivations of deceit. What is hidden can easily be done by others as well as perpetuated by our own selves due to the unwillingness to tap universal knowledge-based systems revealing of much hidden in very plain sight. That which is hidden - enshrouded in the shadows of the unknown and unknowable cannot remain as such. Even more, all things deemed hidden may have been but for a period of time predestined and agreed to in full for the activation of the far future which is now. Oracles prophesied that centuries ahead those of the malevolent side of knowledge would have full yet temporary power and likewise one day cease to widely influence as once before with

11

multitudes of lightbringers, seekers, seers, healers, and activators of the far future in diverse forms/higher mind/abilities and powers never before seen who would emerge. According to these revered visions, the masses would not just find, but reactivate and collectively join the empowering of the present for the future and its forever awakened knowledge. That time, that present, and that future is now! It is time to know and to unlock the many truths of your vibrational knowledge.

The current century of minds will decode, dissolve, and thus do away with old outdated separation, withholding, and/or projecting of misinformation to keep the masses uninformed. The future and every person is likewise easily decodable lending accessible universal truths of self, awareness, and deeper - sometimes intentionally hidden - vibrational understandings. By empowering, this book can therefore enable you and a great many to learn how to decode one of the most powerful symbols within letters. May it be the beginning, the opening of learning and knowledge building that never comes to an end. May you see more than the past and go beyond some of the unwilling present to more concretely activate a deeper state of universal knowingness. Allow the letters, the symbols, the vibrations, the signs, and cosmic frequencies to activate your self, those close to you, the planets, and the multi-worlds within which you, I, and we all live, navigate, and thus coexist.

Naming, Letters, and Vibrational Power

For many, especially the elite and those believed more prominent, they rely heavily on tradition using names as symbolic markers of status and power to be passed down and generationally remembered. Every letter of your name was set into motion vibrationally at birth. No matter if you go by a new name or nickname, you carry vibrations within and all around you simply through each vowel and consonant. Therefore, one, some, and in fact all of the symbols and thus the letters of your name have cosmic influence. When you were named, a vibrational power was unleashed - realized or not. For every name creates certain tendencies, behaviors, destinies as well as life long lessons unbeknownst to many. In having a body each person physically embodies the vibrations set into motion for, through, and by others through naming. This power gains incredible strength through active use - stated, written, and especially via thought (i.e telepathic) - and more importantly through every day, month, year of use on the lived and learned path.

All names are symbolic power influential on patterns of vibrational behavior. You and we all live in the vibrations of what you/we were named - each letter, each vowel, each consonant, the first, the middle, and the last. Therefore, the future of naming matters and will matter significantly more as we all move deeper into a time of global awakening, especially within the current century. The mind, emotions, and the multidimensional self will emerge, evolve, and have greater impact now and even more within the coming future. Naming is critical to that reality for every soul that parts the veil to take a host body and experience a lifepath. The letters of your name, even future children's names are and will remain undeniably pertinent because they create a/many certain futures. In the last and many previous centuries, the giving of same names extended great honor and tradition for at least one or many combined families over generations of time. Yet, as the vibrations climb even higher amid this century of millennial change and massive awakening, the present must come to really understand the vibrational effects and subsequent power of behavior directly set into motion with and through names; the symbology of letters. Giving a child the same name of another or naming children with the same first letter guarantees elements of a shared vibrational future some may want and others may not always prefer or desire. If say 30% of the future named their children after the same actor/musician or the same first letter over and over and over, that/those children will be, will possess, and will at some point on the lifepath collectively act out tremendously similar vibrational behaviors in powerful aspects with great influence/effect on the present/future. Even more, it crafts a particular vibrational future of likeness, even unseen extremes. One of the most common first letters given to an increasing number of children contrary to belief is with the letter "K" as of 2019. With more K letter named children comes unending expression - vocal, creative, and undeniably earth shattering because K lettered people - children and adults - they are known to demand to be heard, to be seen and will do a great deal to not only get ahead, but some will go so far as to invoke chaos in order to get what they want, when and how they want. Knowing the vibrations of letters truly matters.

You can't unknow.

So as names are considered - some beloved, others detested - the present and coming future has greater choice(s) on a/the valued future by knowing most. What you name you, in turn, give as a vibrational gift to the future. Be mindful and ever conscious in the name choice(s) because once given, names can never really vibrationally be altered. With active and continued use they convey an identity, meaning, and cosmic form to the person who symbolically takes on and therefore wears the given/chosen name. Yet, in the universe names are never shed; meaning you can never really be rid of a birth name destined at the beginning on the path. Taking on a new name(s) adds a double or even triple vibration to the person's life and destined evolution that they chose/choose to therefore experience by living with, on, and through it. Vibrations are distinct and letters are symbols that powerfully activate and thus animate a soul by the taking on of a name in this particular life. We are indeed the letters in our names.

We must therefore be ever wise and ever aware in the vibrations we choose for the future. In naming, we give the future what it does, may, and/or may not need. Even casual naming - devoid of any real deeper thought - enables certain frequencies and/or a vibrational evolution future opportunities and options of many kinds to thrive and to navigate the challenges/tests/lessons at destiny's hand. No name, however, is ever really on accident because souls, pre-birth commonly influence name choices from the oversoul so that they can learn in distinctive ways necessary once born to a particular soul path. Your name is apart of your soul DNA and your cosmic makeup.

The future chose you, us all, and is waiting most on greatness through expansion of cosmic knowledge.

Book Goals

There are eight primary book goals within this first of kind learning.

- Introduce the dynamism of symbology
- Show the basics of seeing/reading letters as symbols
- Explore the fundamentals of vibrations and behavior
- Expand the knowledge base of vibrations and cosmic values
- Offer simple cosmic tools to decode yourself, friends, and loved ones
- Reveal the connection of symbols and the four elements of nature
- Access knowledge within multi-worlds of letters & vibrational patterns
- Empower consciousness towards the powerful symbology of names

A B C D E
F G H I J
K L M N
O P Q R S
T U V W
X Y Z

Symbology Letter Keyword Sheet

A - new beginnings, spirit/material fusion, anxiety, high intellect, driven, ambitious
B - nurturing, closed in, emotional intelligence, affectionate, kind, yet sometimes needy
C - great memory, showing towards a new future, open, can often deeply push boundaries
D - doorway, closed in, directed to inner core, secretive, search for deeper alignment
E - forward movement, outward expression, multi-talented, charm, and sharing of emotions
F - rather frank and direct in speaking and living, forward moving, aim for deeper roots
G - divine creativity, musical, artistic, inner power, charm, quiet yet far reaching appeal
H - layered, laddered, bridging, connection, strength, leader, movement, life changes
I - deep, spark, lightning rod of light, illumination, inspiration, universal consciousness
J - youth, sparkling memory, past-life connections, manipulative, cunning, and smart
K - light-bringer, pointed in many directions, able to bridge worlds, often chaotic
L - loving, the point of connection between worlds, high emotions, vibrational sensitivities
M - good with people, management, foundation, peaks and valleys of life, charming, smart
N - bridge for many, having to deal with highs and lows, yet on quest for true path
O - the divine egg, unbreakable, the cosmic mirror, duality, open, and well rounded
P - higher-minded, forward pointed, consciousness, getting rooted, seeing the bottomline
Q - the divine circle, thinks outside norm often otherworldly, very quirky, creative, and fun
R - higher consciousness, divine creativity, can create beauty or fall into lower vibrations
S - transformation, serpent of higher wisdom, multi-worlds, altered paths, sacred mysteries
T - higher mind, can get tied up on ideas, debative, come to crossroads of change in life
U - cup of knowledge, high emotions that can spill over, fun, talkative, striving for balance
V - victorious on path, supreme intelligence, peaks/valleys, connector, open to spirit/life
W - arms stretched to universe, duality, overcoming adversity, lifepath way-shower
X - crossroads, multi-talents, conversations, high emotions, great memory, open sponge
Y - the divine rod, open channel, multiple choices, finding victory of life on a higher path
Z - seeing between worlds, future and past convergences, deeply psychic, high emotions

Decoding Vowels & Consonants

The two primary groups represented among the 26 letters within the English alphabet are *vowels* and *consonants*. Each contain specific vibrations that we/the entire world act out through the letters (separate and combined).

VOWELS = individual, inner state of emotions, where identity is
activated within.

> Vowels decoded are where each person opens to the universe of thy divine self, facing peaks and valleys, sometimes experiencing greatly altered lives that evoke emotion in attempting to find the bridgepoint of life, love, thriving, and most of all transformation. This in short is the cosmic base of your deepest motivations that animates your spirit, soul urges, and lifelong/life living desires. Overall this is the core revelation of self through open emotions that can/will erupt leading to some aspect of profound change.

CONSONANTS = group practical, showing of self/emotions to and
throughout the world

> Consonants decoded represent where and how we show ourselves to the world. Our expression in the everyday world is anchored not only on forward motion and open expression, but ever seeking towards the future. This is where the real you lives as perceived by you, manifested in the way you act, react, fashion yourself and life/style, and where you and we all thus become that which others see. This represents the universal secreted self and the mind of the cosmos and how you express yourself in the world and moving forward. Moreover, this explains how you are driven, fueled, and thus how you help to make the world go round. Through cycles of living we become the bridge of connection to transform the self and to better see the world on deeper levels from all

cosmic perspectives, and to manage change through life, opportunities, and unending universal lessons.

The Cosmic Value(s) of Letters

All letters have a corresponding value, but the deeper side of cosmology includes a numeric value and the root number; meaning more than just one number. The below two charts show the numeric (base) value for each letter in accordance with their placement in the current English alphabet or what some call refer to as the full word total. Each root number (listed, added, and/or thus reduced to) likewise has a vibrational meaning that can give cosmic explanations of the/our behavioral ways of being. The root number in short is a reduced numeric version that correlates with those letters having the same word total and same numerical rate of vibration. They likewise share general basic attributes explored later and throughout this book and vibrationally have great influence in use.

Letters & Numeric Value

A - 1	B - 2	C - 3	D - 4
E - 5	F - 6	G - 7	H - 8
I - 9	J - 10	K - 11	L - 12
M - 13	N - 14	O - 15	P - 16
Q - 17	R - 18	S - 19	T - 20
U - 21	V - 22	W - 23	X - 24
Y - 25	Z - 26		

Letters & Root Numbers

AJS - Root #1	BKT - Root #2	CLU - Root #3
DMV - Root #4	ENW - Root #5	FOX - Root #6
GPY - Root #7	HQZ - Root #8	IR - Root #9

Letters, Symbols & Nature's Elements

All letters resonate with one of the four elements of nature: *Air, Earth, Fire,* & *Water.* As vibrational symbols, each letter projects a distinct frequency that has a core natural element from which it filters out and into the universe/multiverses.

To further enhance the future of symbology from a multidimensional perspective, each letter is listed below with their intuited element so that you and we all can better decode and thus understand the cosmic interplay of the symbology of letters in tandem with one of the four natural elements - life force activators - long respected across many global cultures. Vibrations, especially when read in parallel with nature's elements, become an even more embodied language of the universe and personal being, further underscoring that we are not only our letters, but with diverse letters in words, names, titles, addresses, businesses, and much more, we are made up of and thus activate nature's elements through our being and living.

AIR   (balance, openness, sometimes in the air, go with the flow)
EARTH   (creation, intelligence, grounding, core way of being/expression)
FIRE   (fearless drive, forward movement, raw energy, ignitor)
WATER   (emotions, psychic, unparalleled memory, seeing through illusions)

A - air	B - water	C - air	D - earth
E - water	F - earth	G - fire	H - air
I - earth	J - air	K - fire	L - water
M - earth	N - air	O - fire	P - earth
Q - fire	R - fire	S - fire	T - earth
U - water	V - air	W - air	X - water
Y - earth	Z - water		

Letters & Vibrational Symbolic Groupings

All symbols have a cosmic flow and vibrational patterning that emerges in collective form throughout the twenty-six letters of the alphabet. It is in grouping that you see the connection and patterns of flow that affects everyday behavior. Below the letters are grouped vibrationally as symbols to be seen, read, and universally understood for their similarities.

While many people have names comprised of letters from several groupings, you can and should read according to the first letter (the strongest/highest vibration) as well as the vibrational categorizations revealing many of your/our universal sides. Doing so allows for a closer core read on the who, how, and cosmically why certain evolutions are always in motion. All symbols have codes and deeper meanings to decipher truths for yourself and the many worlds you navigate.

C, L, Z   *"The Seers"*   sight of many kind in the everyday

A, H, M, N,   *"The Seekers"*   climbers, bridge, ladder, walkers

I, J, U, V, W, X, Y *"The Universal Surrenderers"* open to all

F, G, P, R, T *"The Higher-Minded Driven"*   with purpose

B, D, O, Q *"The Inner Doorways"*   multiple layers, divine sight

E, K, S *"The MultiPronged Transformers"* openheart,
                                   highermind

If Letters Had A Symbolic Name

A - The Intelligent Seeker of True Balance
B - The Nurturer of Affection & Innovative Secrets
C - The Seer & Forever Wayshower
D - The Multidimensional Doorways To More
E - The Expressor of Many Creative Prongs
F - The Forward Quest for Higher Foundation
G - The Creative Power of Dimensional Thunder
H - The Climber Bridging Between & Of Worlds
I - The Aligner of Multi-Worlds & Perspectives
J - The Creative Light of Charm & Indecision
K - The Open Rod of Supreme Expression
L - The Passionate Seer of Converging Worlds
M - The Dynamic Mastermind of Multitudes
N - The Ladder of Growth & Universal Expansion
O - The Divine Mirror of Sight and Evolution
P - The Activator of Thought & Forward Change
Q - The Unique Blending of Universal Consciousness
R - The Spark of Creativity & Transformational Fire
S - The Transformer of Soul Wisdom & Ancient Memory
T - The Genius of Debate, Truths & Piercing Perception
U - The Empathic Receptor Of & For The World
V - The Ignitor of Universal Knowledge & Intuitive Victories
W - The Manifester of Inner Wisdom and Freedom
X - The Crossroads of Multi-Conversations
Y - The Divine Rod of Truth & Choices
Z - The Psychic Seer of Deep Emotions

Everyday Letters (A - Z): Decoded & Defined

All letters contain frequencies that flow throughout the planets and the multiverses. Each of the 26 letters are encoded with a distinctly original high vibration. These symbols are also decodable - able to be broken down to basic understanding - in order to advance both practical understanding and active use for learners of any and all kinds. Everyday letters decoded and defined, they show most how the universe expresses itself in/throughout each of us through words, names, people, and all vibrations in the multidimensions; seen/unseen, spoken, thought, written, and understood across the planets. In sum, what follows comprises a first of a kind compilation of cosmic clues to decipher basics of all of the letters revealing: numeric values, destined purpose, keyword characteristics, natural ruling elements and planetary rulings, the opportunities/cosmic tests for learning, as well as showing the vibrational breakdown of behavioral tendencies per letter, per vibration - to truly unlock the symbology of everyday letters.

Bear in mind three key points:

- The 1st letter of any name/word/title is the most amplified and the highest vibration.

- To see the evolution of letters change in symbolism, and most of all showing deep power in written action, see *The Secret Science of Numerology*, especially pages 77 - 137.

- Double/triple or more same letters in a single name/title activates the absolute strongest vibrational frequency through that person, animal, business, home in order to give the deepest learning by living. Bear in mind, this comes with extreme amounts of energy - raw power that flows like a pendulum with extremes on either both, and perhaps for some, all sides.

Aa

"The Intelligent Seeker of True Balance"

Numeric Value: 1   **ONE**
Natural Ruling Element: *Air*
Planetary Ruling: *The Sun*
Vibrational Grouping: The Seekers

Destined Purpose: they come to feel, to experience, to shine through intellect, to empower others, and to find the truth in/through the balancing of self and life

Keyword Characteristics: ever flowing; the bridge/many crosses to bear, hypersensitivity, intelligence, higher mind, finding balance, seeing between worlds.

Whenever Aa is present,

> *The Opportunities:* to see the truth of self, to be the breath of life, be a bridge of knowledge and empowerment, and to activate self expression on high levels.

> *The Lessons/Tests:* learning limits, self control, thinking of self with others, slowing down, activating breath/meditation,

managing life's balance and ever evolving emotions.

A's are the first, they are the adventurers who experience -
many worlds at once and at the same time. They are among the
cosmic group, The Seekers, and likewise begin the vibrational
evolution of all the letters. The letters of the alphabet, framed
outside by an "A" the letter of adventure and knowledge while
ending with depth of sight as a seer with the letter "Z" symbolically
represents the vibrational path of the human experience. Igniting the
first of 25 more vibrations symbologically in place ahead, A's bring
the duality of the higher mind. They are an apex of sorts in one's life
and evolution, crossroads, bridges, walking with higher mind and
purpose while in between the material everyday desires, and the day-
to-day open human world. The A's they empower, given the
heightened depth of knowledge they download, possess, process, and
share even amid the constant motion they always seem to be and to
stay; for balance is a key part of their purpose in any and everything.
To become imbalanced welcomes far greater anxiety for them. Some
are often susceptible to colds and respiratory problems more easily
than other vibrations because their lungs are centrally apart of their
symbology and thus who they are - moving between high and lower
rungs of living - rendering them extremely vulnerable to their
environments affecting their ability to breathe (in life and the
immediate everyday).

As intelligent seekers, they share knowledge while ever
crossing a bridge into even more experiences of great high and great
low vibrations going between the meeting of two worlds, the
interplay of spiritual/universal and material ideas, vibrations, and
ways of being. This letter symbol represents the self standing within
multiple worlds and navigating, seeking, and searching for the point
of contentment or discord even within and of self. Through higher
expression, the apex of life, and outplay of the cosmic plan more
clearly manifests for A's. This energy can, when at the point of
contention/at odds or becoming amplified in any way, it can amass a
collective energy/force able to implode, being often at war with
oneself and or others, detonating in the form of overthinking,
worrying, restlessness, hard to locate or communicate with that can

have great effect at home, the family, community, nation, group, and multi-worlds/dimensions. Being connected to many and or ruled most by the natural element of Air, they move between more spaces, people, and realms where they are intimately connected making them often high sensory, empathic and most of all energetically sensitive. They often stay ever in motion.

The who in the vibrational letter of A depends for a person most on their birthday which together with the remaining letters in one's name forms a soul contract, a blending of vibrations that activates and thus becomes manifested in the wearer of all the vibrations. Symbologically, "A" represents the coming together of worlds for a more perfect balance that is shown through the line in the middle separating the upper spirit realm from the material world gives a balance(ing) of forces or energies to help with the lessons of, in, and through activating balance. Because when unbalanced, the diagonal unique aspects attempt to make an apex/more perfect divine union. Tettering, however, it can/will fall over, disrupt, and it will do so hard, thus with immensely great tests. As such, all A's being open fully to the material everyday therein the social landscape of humans interactions they must seek/live out balance of the mind/body/spirit. Or risk tumbling.

Fully open to many realms at once - as above so below - most A lettered are better at making decisions quickly on the go literally in walking between worlds. That is because of the speed of their minds, much like a flashpoint. They value newness, being first, as they do not want to miss anything most especially originality and unexpected innovation the world can gain; and most times they want to be in charge. They are the breath of life in and of the world and those around them. Therefore fresh air as well as meditation will greatly benefit them in their life evolution, especially in the adult years. They are the breath, the oneness, for their primary path is to understand the secret God power that not only lives within them filtering and therefore empowering the world as a channel, but it manifests/transcends the multiverses even farther being influence with the natural element of Air. This letter is very much the initiator with unrelenting initiative/self reliance and phenomenal willpower. They are more influential as builders and innovators because they often want others to join them and carry out the plan. Therefore, many A's are quite known for beginning many projects, innovating with enthusiasm, but not all are good at finishing or completing projects. So guard against commitments and full expectations of their follow through as some A letters unless balanced with other letters may inadvertently hinder completion of things, projects, and expectations of them. You may be waiting on them more than once. A's without a doubt are charmingly able to achieve success and demonstrate profound intelligence charm & innovation around business ventures and community empowerment for A's always love a crowd, and being seen and heard. Basking in the energy of the sun, they will always and forever shine!

Their life evolving tests will always lie around manifesting, creating new, and having proper balance in the process. Symbolically for them it's about living life standing on two feet, on the path of alignment, and finding unity in one's life. Ambition, strength of character will often engage in full force through empowering others as well as nurturing those who can of course even keep up with them.

While greatly known for initiative, A's can be self-centered, deeply opinionated, sometimes absent-minded and even selfish because they think of self/ego first and most time always. They are a powerful vibration with supreme intelligence and the ability to innovate at creatively high levels. They are at full peak when given the task of fueling activities and opportunities for a new start. Some however always want the feeling of being in charge and the leaders at the helm, therefore some A's they can be passionate, aggressive, pushy, and extremely uptight. If unable to find peace, they do become quite restless in their nature. When unsettling does happen to them, so too come the emotions and even rage as some lose all sense of balance by acting out a multitude of unpredictable expressions. True balance of self/love/being for A's is a lifelong key of learning, surviving, and thriving most of all.

B

Bb

"The Nurturer of Affection & Innovative Secrets"

Numeric Value: 2   TWO
Natural Ruling Element: *Water*
Planetary Ruling: *The Moon*
Vibrational Grouping: The Inner Doorways

<u>**Destined Purpose**</u>: to feel, to hold, to know, to be, and to find joy

<u>**Keyword Characteristics:**</u> caring, sensitive, nurturing, wit, intelligence, and fantastic memory

> **Whenever B is present,**
>> *The Opportunities:* to be smart in the world dealings with others, to gain higher perspective for and from different types of people, to have faith, to be victorious on the path, and to gain deeper insight on the world and manifesting within worlds that we navigate.
>>
>> *The Lessons/Tests:* sharing our emotions, wisely understanding limits and emotional holds on/by others, trust, intuition, learning dynamics of partnership, showing intelligence, being honest, truthful, finding balance and being open.

B's represent the merging of self, the inner worlds, intricate layers, and dual bodies that lie within thy own self. As the second of the letters, here lies more in and of the self, the duality, the mind, partnerships, and heightened fullness of emotions. Vibrationally, it manifests with greater sensitivity and nurturing that comes through great compassion paralleled with hardships. The life path of B's requires learning while living in one's being. B's are among the cosmic group, The Inner Doorways. Connected to both the Moon and natural element of Water, this calls forth a life well of emotions, intuition, empathy, universal compassion, as well as tapping a well of memory meaning and memory making arising from the B vibration. As the second of the letters, it is deeply about the mind of the emotions, deep conversations and finding the bridgepoint within the core wisdom of themselves. Symbolically this particular letter is about the house, the mouth, and the womb collectively speaking to core levels and multi-doorways of living and of having experiences framed around the foundation, finding one's voice, and giving birth to some kind of new (internal/external/rebirth) and or giving birth to many. This vibration is about and depicts nurturing breast much like a mother's bosom, mother's love, healing, peace, and universal restoration of loving and healing. The dividing line between the curved top bottom are about layered interior worlds of self amid changing worlds and multi-worlds where one finds/attempt to find full alignment most. Just being for them is really about embodying the straight line the divine cord from spirit manifesting in the physical, so it literally can, will and is to be.

B letters are often shy, but they embody pure love and often crave affection, emotional attention with/by others - friendships and family. They came to know the meaning of nurturing, comforting, providing for others, and giving of love eternal to find balance with nature. With family for some they may find the home space and giving of the complete self in all the familial, house, and core living security needs demanding and perhaps unending. This vibration is all about the emotional and internal fixed in opinions that tend to be, and to relate more to groups, and thus more than just the self. They rarely like to be alone. Partnerships are a preference with B's where they do very well throughout the lifepath. B's are very hospitable, but immersed in low vibrational elements they can become very selfish in their daily dealings - deeply secretive and quite deceptive - with self/and/or others. Vibrations affect them easily as all the letters, but for B's this operates in a double even multilayered way, with lovers and lasting influence of their dealings with the world and surrounding environments.

As the most closed in double layered vibration, B's very much can get boxed in their own internal matrix. This may seem off putting disconnected or disconnecting for some, but lest we forget how very serious B letters can be often worrying for others and at same time being criticized for holding so much inside. They can become secretive, sneaky, overworry and even become blatant downright liars if their fears of judgment from others are heightened. For being closed within can lead B's to frequent experiences of nervousness, headaches, emotional upsets that only they would know and the close world around them. Greatly influenced by their environment can fuel exceptionally smart minds or low vibrational thoughts and/or treatment of others. They must always be nurtured toward balance, peace, and compassion as well as feel deeply supported on the path of living.

They operate best with and through their mind which functions exceptionally fast along with great wit some can easily tap. They do best and yearn most for strong desire in partnerships and connections with others and the meaning moments made, as well as gaining lessons on patience and serenity of the mind. Their decisions often require or involve others input. Without a doubt B's are most times aware of the other - the need for compassion, a hug, and even healing - more than most. For they have great care for the lonely, abandoned, unseen, overlooked, and dispossessed. Above all, cycles of hidden development and hidden talents can arise through B's in their connection to and for the world - seen and unseen - they shine their brightest when supported/supporting. They are the carers/caregivers of the letter vibrations, emotionally attentive often frequently psychic on the world, its wounds, pains, anxieties, lingering traumas, and complex needs for unconditional love.

Cc

"The Seer & Forever Wayshower"

Numeric Value: 3   THREE
Natural Ruling Element: *Air*
Planetary Ruling: *Jupiter*
Vibrational Grouping: The Seers

Destined Purpose: to show, to see, to learn and to have heart sight on the path.

Keyword Characteristics: open/forward, on the go, see/show, good memory, change bringer/maker, fearless.

Whenever C is present,

> *The Opportunities:* to gain and share wisdom through varied perspectives, be the bridge for others, live and spark creativity, make time for play, learn the path of self expression, and unlimitedness they came to show the world.

> *The Lessons/Tests:* to see more, especially through and with others, finding ways to get more grounded, activating the luck and blessings of themselves, to find alignment, and to always remember to create

C's represent the vibrational evolution back to a tangible open form moving from the closed in nurturing B. The letter C comes to show existence by living. It does so in an apex of openness where things are seen, experienced, and thus come together in much higher expression and understanding. Being both the third vibration and among the cosmic group, "The Seers", C's very much are forward-looking, open to trying and tasting new things and gaining new experiences and memories, especially greater freedom of self expression.

The C's are seers, seekers, and wayshowers. Most exhibit intelligent minds, quick wit, are willing to climb towards desired goals in hopes of exciting experiences, openings, deeper insights, and understandings that propel them forward on the path. They can be a bit conservative, and even guarded in their living as well as their thoughts, but most times they respond deeply to ways to have fun and find their deepest freedom. Self expression is one of their vibrational centerpoints. Ruled by Jupiter and the element of Air indicates great opportunities for big luck, blessings, abundance, but also having big faith in the universe and cosmic more to be provided bountiful on the life path.

Vibrationally C means change that comes with vast openings. They are the open mouth, they love to talk (to others while also being loners who talk most in their heads processing when alone). They are the letter that can let it flow out, having a half moon shape, giving light to the earth. Most times in fact C's are very much open to experiences and seeing the world in a more magnified way often through travel, as their path reflects the symbol which is browed at the higher mind, but also part of an ever open wheel of change/movement/flow. The past, lessons, and living come back much like on a karmic wheel where over time they learn to have non attachments, have full faith on the lifepath, and moreover to be fully honest as things always come back when left undone and/or unresolved. To effectively show and empower with deeper heart sight, they must be ready to learn to be the future way-shower, and to see more from others and through multiple perspectives of living.

Giving light to the earth through their presence, C's have higher energy, they are open and have many talents, love to travel, are deeply inspirational, creative, and imaginative. They can in turn also tend to be too serious, critical of others and even gossip a lot. They are very good with words, happy when they bring smiles to others, and they can also be cunning, self centered, and even cutthroat. They enjoy letting themselves shine. They are artistic, preferring professional work, emotionally C's cannot be held in. Often very psychic though not always aware of it nor forthcoming about such intuitive gifts. Seldomly it can be very hard to know how they feel as they will hide their emotions in plain sight. They have great fluidity of speech/power of words. Scattering of energy, C's are all about seeing, or they can lead to difficulties on the path. Some are good at saving money and others live fully in freedom willing to risk the need to save money. Many live in dualities, giving to the world, while closed many times to those around them, thus shielding and setting unique boundaries within and from the world. They love to adorn themselves, appreciate nice looking clothes, are very creative, and are multi-talented - when of course if/when they want you to know. Being good with words, they love great debates, having the last word, and they tend to remember all of what's been said. They come truly to show many a multitude of things and deeper core living with freedom of self.

D

Dd

"The MultiDimensional Doorways to More"

Numeric Value: 4 FOUR
Natural Ruling Element: *Earth*
Planetary Ruling: *Uranus*
Vibrational Grouping: The Inner Doorways

Destined Purpose:to be/experience many doorways of life, to see, and to greatly know a lot.

Keyword Characteristics: universal, highly empathic, sensitive, curious, deeply knowledgeable, great memory, super intelligent, and emotional

Whenever D is present,

The Opportunities: to hold the key to forward movement, to be smart, to find roots, gain multisight/perspective, to use and harness emotions, to create, and find times to activate joy.

The Lessons/Tests: to enjoy self and to find balance in guarding against selfishness, to show emotions in smart ways not to overdo it, to oppose manipulation and low vibrational engagement, to be the higher ground, and remain relentless in the climb towards their goals and desires.

D's represent the place in the vibrational evolution that is about the multidimensions and inner crossroads that emerges after the expressive way showing that C invites, the letter D conversely is the higher mind that gives birth to doorways much like a womb. They are the womb/world openers who understand the way to gain stability if because they are ever on a quest of the mind and freedom of living. They are among The Inner Doorways. Connected deeply to the electrifying planet Uranus and the natural element of Earth points to practicality and quick intelligence that is direct and will spark expansion that could even lead to a world wide embrace of thoughts, innovation, songs, books, and much more.

As the 4th of the letters, D's are/about the crossroads. They often endure, confront, and even bring crossroads into other people's lives. For themselves crossroads and confrontation with the inner core self will be lifelong and for some, significant deaths may happen around them that can be traumatizing for some, the holding of latent grief for others and/or even the remaking of themselves through a death of an old self amid major transformations. They are the keyhole and key holders. They come vibrationally to surrender and most to find and activate faith in self and others. Having faith in themselves, and the worlds around them is critical because through tests/crossroads comes a reset in the heart to find deeper foundations that can fuel them forward. In going through and seeing so much they become a doorway to and for many inner worlds often never imagined. Seeing, hearing, and knowing a lot, they are quite often high sensory empaths deeply intuitive in thought and of feeling what may be coming, the best way to move forward on the path, and even having psychic clarity about people.

D's are deep thinkers. Their thoughts dwell in deep waters of being as the most curious, ever taking swift dives for greater understanding. They likewise hold keys for the world around them to find greater significance in their lives. They are universal manifesters able to easily create, are fast thinkers who have great memories to rely on, and they believe in family and their roots. Their family can be a great source of inspiration, joy, need, and even pain in the living evolution. They love a good time but they also are smart in guarding against spending over time with the world in order to make and take time for self. A great many in fact love to be alone and can become selfish with their time if really permitted. Although well-meaning, their life intention is to find life balance so as not to become moving on the rocker they are partly anchored wherein which they tend to stay in, remain closed, and sometimes show very little emotion causing manipulative holding of deep dark secrets that some will carry to the grave.

Symbolically D's represent the womb/door between worlds. Shutting things in, they sit firmly on the line so its a letter of balance, half moon that has greater point of convergence and alignment where all things come together through the many doorways. They are on the path to become and most to be tested towards destiny's rise through sometimes unfavorable circumstances. Driven to prevail above sometimes great hardships, they can become workaholics which gives a focus for the channeled energy greatly held within. For them seeing is believing so hardwork matters on high levels. When you meet them some can be opinionated, ultraconservative, gloomy, straightlaced, argumentative, stubborn, many more however are fair, honest, trustworthy, dependable, fun, and anchored very much on depth of knowledge, cracking codes, conspiracies, abundance, and most of all securing a long term foundation. Their greatest lesson is about moving through changes and therefore knowing the proper balance necessary for their everyday personal lives of thriving above all else.

E

Ee

"The Expressor of Many Creative Prongs"

Numeric Value: 5   FIVE
Natural Ruling Element: Water
Planetary Ruling: Mercury
Vibrational Grouping: The Multipronged Transformers

Destined Purpose: to have many experiences, to produce, to create, and to remain forward moving even unbound by others demands and societal expectations.

Keyword Characteristics: expression on high levels (inside and external) always on the go, deep intelligence, charming, and three pronged in nature.

> **Whenever E is present,**
>> *The Opportunities:* to see the future with higher perspective, to find and live alignment, to be victorious on the path following great peaks and valleys, and most to see the self in fully expression and find value for the multi-chapters of one's life.
>
>> *The Lessons/Tests:* to surrender to the universe, to guard against anxieties, and find balance, peace of mind and meditation, to activate intelligence, know limits, and to always activate balance life-work-play

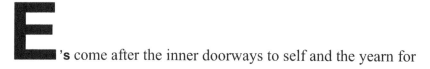

E's come after the inner doorways to self and the yearn for freedom and outward expression regrows in the vibrational evolution of the letters. This letter activates change and stays forever on the forward path of movement often in multiple directions. They are of the highly expressive kind! Freedom through adventure, multi-experiences, they are the letter outstretched, open to unique and varied vibrations that enhances life and its meaning for them. They come to get, give to the world, and also to receive. Being among the cosmic grouping, "The MultiPronged Transformers" they greatly transform the lives of those around them and close in the life path because of the layers and dimensions and varied ways of being that they are, carry and project. As the 5th letter, freedom, forward going, mobility, multitudes of experiences and being open to trying and therefore knowing more deeply is inherent to the letter E. It will matter greatly at different points in/on the life path and yet through aspects of their entire life. Their arms and aims are towards the future indicating a profound attunement within them that allows knowing how to be and also how to operate in certain circles, dealings and with certain people that others may not get, or ever gain access to. E's express and they need/understand expression in and of the world most and best.

Ruled by Mercury, Es are ever active and have very smart minds while tied with the element of Water suggesting that they operate out of deep emotions, they have experiences that often can activate strong emotional intelligence and profound intuition, wherein which they just know the best way, right person to meet, and/or road to take, etc. Being a 5th letter similarly explains vibrationally how and why E's are always on the move and for them survival seems to come when needed most no matter the obstacle. They can see the future, have an impeccable memory, and may have alternate perspectives and varied personalities even acted out to outsmart others in order to get their way.

They are symbolically open with many prongs and significant aspects to their core character that comes with profoundly high expression that will always manifests in a variety of ways. E's are very deep, love to talk, sing, speak, love, make music, sex, they are the letter of communication, words, and true self expression. They are open all around so they tend to have a greater sense of freedom and willingness to try new things. some can have a nervous temperaments and even split personalities. E's are open to try, test, and taste everything which can also lean towards overdoing it because they are so open. They are also deeply affectionate. However lower energy E's can be cold as ice. Generally E's are extraverted yet often a quite changeable vibration where they will frequently change their minds and moods when you least expect. They are immensely expressive. Many are progressive, some may have metaphysical interests as well as material world pursuits. Often they are more worldly than spiritual, yet those that seek higher philosophical ideas expand profoundly in ways often unseen. Lower energy E's however can be vocally critical of others and at times exhibit a strong temper, have a propensity to lie, steal, and/or find themselves getting in trouble with the law; perhaps even more than once. They are an energetic and restless vibration always driven by the lingering lure of their universal purpose(s) and living most in their envisioned abundance of freedom to express.

F

Ff

"The Forward Quest for Higher Foundation"

Numeric Value: 6   SIX
Natural Ruling Element: *Earth*
Planetary Ruling: *Venus*
Vibrational Grouping: The Higher-Minded Driven

Destined Purpose: to feel, to know, to find and give grounding, to have faith, and be fearless on the lifepath

Keyword Characteristics: frank, direct, forward moves/moving, integrity, roots, friends, and family

Whenever F is present,

The Opportunities: to experience, move through life and several transformations, to find alignment, to express themselves, and to survive even challenging crossroads.

The Lessons/Tests: Understanding balance through expression, be a spark and believe in change, be the change activator, maintaining higher ground and understanding life's climb to include helping connect to and with others.

F 's represent what comes after all the changes, the freedom giving experiences widely sought and activated by E. This vibration emerges after the realm of multi-experiences and the plunge into freedom, bringing a more browed conscientious letter frequency. They love a good time and are ever forward moving yet with the higher mind and philosophies, the family, their version of freedom, the body, alignment, forging roots, and seeing between worlds of precision, and clarity of direction which matters a great deal to them. F's embody forward movement on the life path of evolution. They are among "The Higher Minded Driven" and rightfully so because they are vital assets to those around them if permitted closeness with them. Their minds, often in many deep terrains of intelligence, they seldom forget anything, any person met, date set, while they always have incredible discernment into future realms of possibilities, risk, and opportunities. They most times are genuinely the visionary ones able to see/map the coming future. They are concerned very much with their communities, their friends and families, they also understand law and order often seeking to uphold it within personal life even becoming conservative, rigid, detailed oriented overbearing at times than their peers. Some are drawn to politics, others move towards counseling, and teachers/professors. F which is a 6 number energy represents the voice that must be heard, it is no surprise therefore so many often go into public or motivational speaking. They are most fulfilled when they accomplish things that are for others. Some people may enter a field of music, writing, decorating, acting, military and/or performing, which is at its essence serving others.

Naturally graced with the ability to maintain a higher perspective, as the 6th letter, they represent the body, higher mind, and spirit but even more the voice that must be heard especially with speaking and or writing. Always concerned about their core communities, some even lean to politics, counseling, finance and entrepreneurial routes, or teachers/professors where their leadership capabilities can fully expand with institutions. When they take on responsibilities they do so seeing it as their civic duty. They will be efficient with the follow through without very little prodding necessary. F's also carries a double cross where many people come to them with their problems and they, in turn, will in short "carry the load" with genuine affection and compassionate meaning. While others do come to them, being two-pronged and able to tip/topple over, they can become unbalanced and for some even unhinged. They need calm and prefer to avoid confusion and drama, but if sparked they will loudly and quickly hold their own with the swiftness of mind and body often unseen in others. Most times F's want to finish things and to do so in peace.

Symbolically, F's are the arms outstretched, forward, and future-facing. This is symbiotic of them being outstretched to help those near them. 6 energy is highest and best when and through service. They are most fulfilled when they accomplish things including those for others. They have a natural higher perspective, open mind, heightened sixth sense, and are very loving, open at the heart. Their sight between worlds is almost unparalleled and because of higher brow and mind ever future facing. Through it, they are gifted with deeper sight and vastness of sight from multi-perspectives. They likewise are even more influenced by the intergalactic combination of love, luxuries, beauty with Venus as well as an element of Earth indicating that they love deeply - the work, the people, their passion, and they can also be the grounding, the energy of creation that while sometimes dry and reserved in nature, can affect masses. Some, in fact, do equally understand and believe the power they possess once in full balance. They are the vibration that being immensely powerful, they are able to move with the ease of universal delight of self with and in of the world. The programs of the higher mind, core breath of life/self, are open, expressive, roots, family, freedom, and focus. Above all else, this vibration is forward bound and ever forward moving with practical vision of success.

G

Gg

"The Creative Power of Dimensional Thunder"

Numeric Value: 7   SEVEN
Natural Ruling Element: *Fire*
Planetary Ruling: *Neptune*
Vibrational Grouping: The Higher-Minded Driven

Destined Purpose: to harness creativity, honor their genius, activate art on profound levels; appeal to many and thus to find one's destiny

Keyword Characteristics: Smooth, psychic, creative, artistic, even magical in life and production

Whenever G is present,

The Opportunities: to be wise, a way-shower through transformative experiences, to express yourself and inner core, to be victorious in life and creations, to show many sides of thy self, to be the bridge of, for, and to many.

The Lessons/Tests: learning how to harness inner fire, (seen/unseen) to find alignment, to be expressive, open yet guarded against lower vibrations that could cause the path of addictions and indulgence.

G's are the profoundly sacred vibration that comes after the deep conscientious plunge to understand self in and of the world that came before with F. The G's come to be transformed, to activate through transformation unseen, and to bestow higher understanding for others. In many ways they parallel the vibration of letter C, however anchored with at least horizontal and vertical symbolic angles pointing to the core and a bridge of the divine self, the embody layers of dimensional and creative power ever flowing - both within and externally to the multiverses. Symbolically they represent a C yet with a hook pointed inward and up indicating openness that G's both channel and process in truly profound ways. Uncoiled within the higher mind and looked at from the evolutionary scale, as the 7th letter they are and come to invoke the sacred; of self in and of to the world. They are the letter symbolically of deeper introspection and one's life ever aligned with an almost impenetrable inner core because of the vibrational abilities and powers they possess and know full well how to harness towards their desired need(s). G's are among "The Higher Minded Driven" alluding to dynamic intelligence, and knowing how best to see the higher perspective while also how to navigate many worlds and many people. Neptune ever shaping their magnetic field, they are here to activate magic within themselves while likewise seeing through and past illusions/delusions of self and others and/or the evolving world around them.

They are the sacred fire that lies prominently among all the letters. Gs therefore emit sacred unique aspects of living that being deeply spiritual and often religious seeking, they possess innate abilities to connect always with truth, divine creativity and how to be universal in their living. In essence, there is limitless depth to them they always yearn for and are attracted to in and on their personal lifepath and through it they have the ability to manifest and make things happen almost as if by magic while staying open to the outpouring of the universe in their everyday life. They are the greatest magicians among us, sometimes holding close to the source of their alchemical knowingness. How they apply these unique gifts/varies from writing, music, acting, reading, and or serving in the role of advising others. The dimensional power of their mind allows access to inner circles far unattainable by others. Multi-talents of high proportion lie sometimes intellectually hidden from public sight until they are ready. This energy correlates within G's inner power that is the focus of the evolving path of life and its prevailing mysteries.

Many G's can be social yet frequency they are withdrawn, preferring the solitude or observers stance when among others preferring themselves and their minds. Solace enables the unlocking of greater mysteries intriguing and or puzzling to them when distractions are at a significant minimum. They speak well, in fact beautifully - words, voices, and the throat being supreme and or even their greatest test on the path. They are however not always as talkative as the other letters. G's tend to keep their own counsel, can be secretive or even distant with others while often more concerned with their own wellbeing, and dreams than others. They love their family and keep loyal close ties with friends. They can likewise be reserved, opinionated, sarcastic, strong willed, aloof, even morbid, use brutal words being sometimes ever on the endless quest to solve hidden meanings and understand people's motives. Spiritually they are often admired and looked up to for their willpower and deep wisdom. They tend to be considered an upstanding great inspiration for humankind and often groups around them. Moreover, their path is focused on self searching, analysis, deep thinking in the quest for inner peace and most of all tapping their universal knowledge.

H

Hh

"The Climber Bridging Between & Of Worlds"

Numeric Value: 8   EIGHT
Natural Ruling Element: *Air*
Planetary Ruling: *Mars*
Vibrational Grouping: The Seekers

Destined Purpose: to climb, to have unique experiences, to see between worlds, and to be a creative bridge for many.

Keyword Characteristics: charm, strength, endurance, intelligence, balance, empowering and ever moving on life's spectrum.

Whenever H is present,

The Opportunities: to find your power, learn through the multitude of experiences, to see varied perspectives, be the effect point of alignment, to be the divine spark of creativity, to move through and show genius truth and to allow experiences to enable climbing to higher levels.

The Lessons/Tests: to guard against anxieties, not overreacting, to learn proper limits and when best to say no, to be a changemaker, and to learn the balanced value of play and hardwork.

H's are the vibration that opens back to the universe although they come to climb and move between worlds more than any other vibrational letter. Through the shifts, changes, and endless twists and turns, they see the bridge point of connection, disconnection, and where even disrepair and changes are necessary. They come to learn and through it they elevate with and towards empowerment and full understandings of others. Symbolically they are patterned similar to F as well as to letter I which points towards openness, moving between rungs and realms, having open ears/open hearts, being willing to navigate duality and even massive changes while remembering to establish and even re-establish the roots of thy self and foundational core with friends, family, and groups that matter in their close personal lives. Some could argue that letter H symbolically is made up by two letter I's joined at the heart of connection for H is the rung of activation, fully embodying the concept of lifting as they climb on the lifepath.

More than any other letter, as they climb they empower and inspire those around them. Many others see H's as leaders, authority, one able to align in more innovatively creative ways than some others who dwell in uncertainties and unwillingness. Being universally anchored with elements of "Air", they are curious and led by their multi-talents and interests. They are unafraid to be or to journey alone in the quest for deeper knowledge often through roads far less traveled thus underscoring their being among "The Seekers". They stand on two portals pointed up high and down below and through them the future can and will manifest, transcending any assumption of meager averageness. Mars fuels their passion, their fearless ambition, and their drive for greater and the far deeper/transformative.

They are givers to those close around them. They do things many times for the core family/unit often serving to be the bridge of higher ground for the future. Therefore they are often unbothered by the solo path or taking the road less traveled. They must have shared energy in the giving and receiving however because they can topple and go deep with heightened emotions and or even overindulgence. H's likewise must always seek ways of proper balance with food, meditation, nature in their life to further center their body, mind and spirit and future enlightenment for they are a vital key to change for global masses. Some may move between worlds until roots become entangled that gives rise to the new between far many worlds and dimensions than ever imagined.

They are a life giving force and they are the activators. H's are the ladder with, to and even arguably multidirectional where they can always vibrationally flow up and down - therein through highs and lows. They like us all also have choice of descension into negative and ascension into positive choices thoughts and deeds. Having the numeric connection of eight, they come to find, to be, and thus to activate their power. They will do so and become closely entangled with others while being a central beacon looked upon by a massive global many. Through it, the hardships they use, find and through it reactivate their power that always permits greater opportunities through the cycles. They must continually put forth effort for every penny and guard against careless spending. They however tend to use good judgment and operate as the humanitarian traveling the world with significant humanitarian impulses and interests. Good health is critically important for physical coordination and effectively balancing for life to harness their emotions, especially learning to control their temper. They can become extreme expressives at turning points that they deem necessary. They must therefore hold close to the influence of their speech because the power of their words and vibrational presence is dimensional and far reaching perhaps more than even they realize. Being mindful of the influence of words/speech and long term ideas help to prevent the great behavioral tendency some H's have to abuse words. When in debates and or heated arguments their worlds can invariably cut deep. H's overall they give, they renew life, and they are a critically pertinent healing energy, and higher frequency that comes to exact new power for the collective and future good.

I

Ii

"The Aligner of Multi-Worlds & Perspectives"

Numeric Value: 9   NINE
Natural Ruling Element: Earth
Planetary Ruling: Neptune
Vibrational Grouping: The Universal Surrenderers

Destined Purpose: to hear, to know, to understand, to balance, and to empower in multiple directions.

Keyword Characteristics: balance, life alignment, survival, and refinement of the mind.

Whenever I is present,
> *The Opportunities:* experience multitudes, survive peaks and valleys; to be and to find alignment, to experience the self amid others.

> *The Lessons/Tests:* to show thy full self, to be a balance and guard against imbalances, to abstain from low vibrational pull, to create in many directions, and to learn the deeper meaning of hard-work and lack thereof.

I's are the creative vibration, they represent
reproduction/alignment. They embody spirit descending into matter as a living soul of and bearing light of the universe. This vibration above all is regarding by ancient mystics as the higher self, the god within, the full dimensional self, and also the ego. I's are here to active inner strength, to bring to the world the small voice and light within. Many strive for perfection perhaps knowing within their subconscious that they come to bring and even to become more. They are among the "The Universal Surrenderers" which points to the need for full faith, acceptance, and alignment of self and letting go of that which does not serve them. Some find the life challenge of letting go easier than some others where attachment can be a key theme that they came to relearn/release and dwell in faith and restoration of self.

Their eyes, ears, and heart are fully open literally and symbolically. In many ways they are walking portals channeling and downloading - everyday, and most especially for some I's in dreams. Coming through this vibration to have an eye for much, they are not only high sensory, but they are the pole, the activator, the lightning rod of life and enlightenment and transformation. As a result they can evoke higher emotions and greater sensitivities to the world. Far from any small vibration they tend to hold strong opinions because lest we forget they came to see and to create but they also very much came to be heard. Serving as a consummate rod and beacon of light they must do more than receive but likewise give to the worlds around them.

Emotions and alignment matter deeply as all I's look to master themselves and learn themselves, strategies for survival, forging future legacies, and having total reliance on their divine personal abilities. They are the wayshowers and forward marchers. Their path brings to bear the need to be thoughtful in love in and of the world - to themselves remembering self care, proper balance, gratitude, compassion and understanding through multi-perspectives. I's many times can serve as the middle point, the mediator, listener, and or they can indeed be a live wire affecting all within close proximity. This owes to the universal reality of - as above, so below, and all around - thus they are the only letter that is fully open at every turn, symbolically making them fully open to the outside vibrational external world. How it manifests of course depends on their life path and point of awareness and or deeper awakening to who and how they are energetically made up and vibrationally comprised.

Ruled by Neptune, I's come to activate their magic, to see through and in between illusions and moreover to activate realities they deeply desire. Most have a strong sense of balance on earth, maybe too much, as some can be rather dry, conservative, detached while others are deeply sensitive to the needs of others, even to their detriment. Being unable to know and balance boundaries and the need for divine alignment of self and staying forward moving will arise many times on the vibrational journey. With number 9 ever shaping their cycles of life, they are capable of finishing things well if and when they surround themselves by high vibrational people/living and lifestyles. While also letting go and letting the Universal/Divine. They also gain through higher mastery of unconditional love - deeper energy about letting go and anchoring into true self. The challenges will test through the overtun, the topple, and the dismay that vibrationally will propel to learn trust, faith, and knowingness of truth. I's walk between multi-worlds and multi-perspectives ever on the divine quest to align, survive, and most to empower - themselves/the evolving mind.

J

Jj

"The Creative Light of Charm & Indecision"

Numeric Value: 10   TEN
Natural Ruling Element: Air
Planetary Ruling: Saturn
Vibrational Grouping: The Universal Surrenderers

Destined Purpose: to feel, to understand, to invoke change, to create, to inform and thus to empower multitudes in many directions.

Keyword Characteristics: movement, balance, higher mind, decision/indecision, past, life, enlightenment

Whenever J is present,

> *The Opportunities:* using the higher mind to express yourself, to be the bridge, and to see through points of indecision, navigating life's peaks and valleys, and to find balance working hard with the mind harnessed.

> *The Lessons/Tests:* the need for honesty, seeing through all sides, guarding against impulsivity and indecision, rechanneling the outplay of hypersensitivity; to invoke smart restraint; to effectively manage the mind, emotions, and any anxieties.

J J's are a light force, a divine rod of high-level consciousness,

universal understandings, as well as uncertainties. They are vibrationally patterned similar to I letters although emblazoned with a hook moving back and forth open, flowing and deeply unpredictable on the path and full way of being going forward. They are the universe that exists nestled within humanity, much like a master among the global many. However, the cosmic catch is that some and many have been before being tasked now with new paths to explore, learn from and through. Yet not all see or even remotely believe they come to learn more from lessons of the past/past lives. Some may assume averageness about themselves but they are past life connected - in abilities, emotions, talents, however with that they lie ever on the cross of choices, where life shows them responsibilities that they can choose to sway back and forth with uncertainty or swim with clarity focus and direction. They come in to activate and become embodied with supreme high vibration. The cross and crown symbolically is in and of them as some J's are religious more than others. Some J's likewise move between and carry lifepath of deeper inner conflict on religious choice and spiritual activation, trying to be the balancer between people, worlds, expectations, and coming nuanced vibrations.

J's are a deeply intense frequency. As masters walking they have incredible psychic abilities that strengthen exponentially when they let go of old ideas and appeasing expectations of and for others. They come to let go, lose parts, and gain even stronger parts that lead them back to a holistic balance. They are drawn to the mystic, universal mysteries, higher philosophies and spiritual enlightenment with practical revelation. Materially and spiritually they also full of high aspiration, which time, life and evolution will prove necessary to develop in profound ways. Sometimes even untapped and therein latent abilities and power they can easily harness. Most J's in addition to profound charm and magnetic appeal, they are typically and honest, benevolent, brilliant, and deeply intuitive. Age and maturity brings core experiences and wisdom unattainable for some and even many. They are hardworkers wherein which they can and many will be outstanding in their work. Although they may hide innate fears of failure and uncertainty on choices/decisions made, they are clever, and equipped with good memory, powerfully good at retaining knowledge evidenced by being hooked pointed to the past. Their cup of memory runs deep so never think you will let much past them because brilliance permeates even the J's who may seem gullible. With charm innate and hooked to the past also invites cunning, ever youthful, ever playful energies for some bordering on immature and irresponsible. J's love to play. Being open and among the cosmic group. "The Universal Surrenderers" they let go and they can let a lot in. Therefore balance is exponentially key. Low vibrational J's are known to be liars, thieves, manipulators laced with an incredible charm that can fool even the most cautious. They are and can be the joker/actor/musician and fraud. They seldom ask for advice and direction relying on intuition, and trying to outsmart and outwitting the unsuspecting other rendering it impossible the direction of their mind and/or actions. High vibration J's transform many lives, while those steeped in base materializing will thrive most in lies they lived most that invites and invokes full chaos.

J's stay on the go embodying the rocker they are. They give a feeling of well being with/to others but they are also plagued with much higher anxieties, unseen, chronic health issues and employing dishonesty in the moments they deem necessary. They are witty, humorous, and really fun to be around. Most of course only with those willing to show playful side make time for fun. When they tap intuitive capabilities to rely on self, drawing on God force within, the stage is not only there for them, they too become the stage through acquisition of higher knowledge. They can easily work with others. They will also stay up late many nights more than their peers to know and to be deeply informed. They are the cross, the crown and the enacted alignment of Universal/God's power which in turn makes possible for the high vibrational living, an ennobled and for some advanced position of higher authority/life. Above all else, J's come to be the master to and of the world and most to shine light on the future here and coming of more. Permanently anchored in the numeric vibration of 10, they are the stage, seeing the self through the cosmic mirror, showing and manifesting an impact on dimensional masses as inspiration and other entangled learning of how best to live a life of higher vibrations. The choice, stage, and activation lies within J's to chose the path that serves them best to light the future way to their happiness.

K

Kk

"The Open Rod of Supreme Expression"

Numeric Value: 11 ELEVEN
Natural Ruling Element: Fire
Planetary Ruling: Double Vibration of The Sun
Vibrational Grouping: The Multipronged Transformers

Destined Purpose: to give, to feel, to become empowered, to find one's voice, to find balance of emotions.

Keyword Characteristics: multitudes, expressive, open, debate, conversation, lightning rod

Whenever K is present,

The Opportunities: to express, empower on high levels that can influence world, to be a bridge for many, show love, to overcome great obstacles, and to show multiple talents and experiences, climb and be a wayshower to others.

The Lessons/Tests: to balance emotions, remain forward moving, be unbothered by others gossip/external views, walk in self truth, to shine, to find emotional balance, and to learn great compassion.

K's are the lightbringers hooked on supreme expression of many kinds. If J brought in a vibration of uncertainty, then letter K is precise, direct, sharp in profoundly immense ways. They embody divine love and great love for humanity expressed predominantly out within the world. Without a doubt where there is a letter K, they will be seen and/or more than likely heard. Vibrationally K is many things and representatives of opportunities on the lifepath to activate, evolve, and learn from. They are masters and they come to master many things, utilize incredible opportunities, to be victorious on the path even through what may seem unending peaks and valleys that bring obstacles and overtunage on the winding life path. Yet they/their story/multiple stories of survival are inspirations to many and within many realms and dimensions. They hold and carry the lighted torch speaking truth to the world in direct yet even unique ways and means for some even downright odd and misunderstood ways that still can appeal and electrify. They bring light to the world, laughter, joy, surpassing impossibilities taking and activating opportunities when granted freedom of full self.

As a double vibration of the Sun, K's undoubtedly come to shine beyond the here and now, they come to shine and be the fire of light and deeply passionate expression; because Fire rules them. When provoked they can overcome mountains while likewise bring down a forest in one fell swoop with the innate fire of thought, words, and inspiration of being that they carry and express in continually seen and unseen aways. In a dimensional sense they are akin to dragons steeped in centuries of magic and likewise unashamed to breath fire on direct targets of their mind and emotion to illuminate truth and new beginnings. Because of the multiplicity of their divine talents, they are rightfully among the cosmic group of letters "The MultiPronged Transformers" those who are infinitely more than they may seem, coming with profound great purpose breathing fire into new beginnings that will not only appeal and appease groups, Ks as masters of words, storytelling, truth-bearing as well as disseminating information very far and wide. As a numeric value of eleven, they are the illuminative they also continuously walk between many worlds/portals and multiverses, serving as the information bringer and way showers. They more than any other letter embody double vibrations, two in fact (from the Sun and number 11) meaning when sparked/triggered their vibrations are earthshaking and powerfully influential within and around the worlds in which they operate and dwell deep in thought and mind. For they walk through many worlds, giving and absorbing illumination all the time.

Symbolically K's are the evolution of the self, and the mouth open to the future, an open self, speaking to and through multiple worlds, higher vibrations, dimensions that electrifies more than the mere seen. Combined with other letters this double amplified vibration can bear resemblance to the dragon (powerful transmitter of fire/transformative truth) among us all. They are symbols of holding and taking hold of opportunities, those things received. Their success depends most on how they use their talents. Things can quantify and come easily to them but if and how they operate fully on ego/part of themselves they block being the channel and transmitter for the world. K's can be overly sensitive, some dishonest, operating with hidden motives and intense secrets, they can be unsympathetic, sneaky, and deeply narrow minded. Yet most often they are charismatic, electrifying, divine rods of supreme expression, multi-talented with an ability to learn quick and fast sometimes without extensive classroom and traditional learning. They are masters of information who come to relearn themselves as powerful teachers and lifelong students within and of the multidimensions. Symbolically within the letter K, the upper part is downside up as a V and upside down lower part with its feet firmly planted on the ground, revealing even more how it filters receives energy - as above so below. One side of K is giving and there is an openness of self to all thereby filtering energy outward in full expression in and to the future. Whereas the other part is about the every deep person and managing the house of self and creating a foundation and long term legacy. The straight line in a divert anchor/angle rod to the higher dimensions and the need to get feet firmly planted on the ground/rooted/deeply anchored.

As powerful beings, K's need music to calm the vibration and give inspiration. When it allows the light to shine it emanates dynamism to other people. At any parts of the imbalance and or complete overturn, symbolically it invites not only chaos but an emotionally fragmented self that can go deep and internal with long range consequences where they mentally can appear on and off as the void attempts to hold the self imprisoned within delusions and multiple realities. Knowledge expression more than all of other themes will forever predominate K's path and they therefore should be nurtured to allow the duality and multiplicity of talents and ways of being and activating knowledge giving that is necessary in order for them to manifest more. They are massive light bringers tasked with great purposes and most especially illumination of high proportion in, of, and for the vibrational future.

L

Ll

"The Passionate Seer of Converging Worlds"

Numeric Value: 12 TWELVE
Natural Ruling Element: Water
Planetary Ruling: Jupiter
Vibrational Grouping: The Seers

Destined Purpose: to love, to feel, to be the connector, to be apart, to open, to find life-balance

Keyword Characteristics: open, bridgepoint, expression, creativity, many, multitudes, connection.

Whenever L is present,

The Opportunities: to be the bridge, to see the bridgepoint to and for other, to surrender, have faith, find balance in self expression and self love, be victorious on the path and to create on high levels.

The Lessons/Tests: to let go the need for control, to find life and self balance especially of emotions, to guard against indecision and living on an explosive rocker, to use intellect wisely, to have balanced perspective, to know the best way toward high vibrational living.

L 's are the vibrational blending of worlds of the self and the universe to create a more perfect, pure, raw energy comprised of great highs and great lows. Following illumination of information and universal expression with K comes the merging of the self within open worlds and multiverses that L activates and is activated by. It is the strongest and purest vibration. L's they are love and as such they love incredibly hard, feel immensely, and see through to more and between worlds, places, and people of a deep passion. L's are exceptionally powerful, unique, compassionate, and endearing. They mean what they say and what they say - written, said, and or thought - and what they in fact say will be heard and very likely also felt. They are the connectors to and through much. Cosmically they are among "The Seers" the ones who come to give and receive, to create experience, to feel and learn most through human experiences.

They live their lives in and at constant bridges and life-points meaning that for the L vibration the self always stands next to the world through unending opportunities and choices. The self is always on the quest for deeper foundation and alignment on the forward move in ways both seen and unseen. Being equal only with letter I, as an open vibration that L's are, they hear everything around them making them highly sensitive, some extremely high sensory with heightened perception and intuition, and absolute supreme expression - whether external or internal. Without a doubt L's are of a highly evolved vibrational sensitivity. Their baseline extends further out between and from themselves, they are caregivers, protectors, providers, and the ones who carry many, going through a lot, maybe being one of many or or giving birth to many children, or perhaps the one who takes on greater burdens, longer harder walks than peers and siblings. Symbolically this vibration also points to vocalizing of self to the outside world in profound ways that touches the hearts of many, especially in fashion, oratory, technical skills, and/or even the written word. In many regards they are a V at an angle and pointed to the multi-worlds of heaven and earth thus amid peaks and valleys, they will not only overcome, but they will prove victorious on the path perhaps more than once in even unusual ways. Invariably L's come here to express many avenues of themselves perhaps even living through some divergent and or drastically altered lives that take them in new directions and exceptional new ways and routes.

Being ruled by the planet Jupiter, luck and blessings come to them easy, however so too do big things in life. Some even come from big families. The family, core, unit of love surrounding personal life matters greatly to them. Some L's may experience full immersion of love while others endure complete exile and or separation from kin for divine reasons. With water the natural element of their vibration, they feel and very deep, being often unusually emotional, even angry and cantankerous. For a great many who may not even realize they act out deep psychic intuitive abilities that often increases with age and awareness. They see beyond what others do and/ or do not, they try to remember a lot, and they can often see through to what others shield and/or hide in their secret lives.

L is for loving, learning, and living. L makes up one of the four vibrations for this powerful universal word called LOVE. Many L's are therefore romantic in nature and devoted to their family. They are vibrationally who they are. Therein, many L's can be warm expressive, generous, romantic, and loving but when upset they can become frigidly cold and very off-putting. They are very sensitive in nature, and highly creative and attuned to the universe. Unlike other vibrations, they do not rock or scatter most times, so they are less impulsive. But some may also be open in that precise way of being deeply passionate and explosively intense energy wise that in fact fuels a necessary core of life long learning, most times starting at childhood. L's likewise are very open to receiving good and tends to have a wise approach in life. Often some have higher sexual desires/drives. They are not always spontaneous some even preferring a more routine oriented life to reduce the chaos of the mind/living. Their base is straight and will not move as quickly so they tend to think before acting while some act out emotionally opposite thinking later on the effect caused on others. This letter has highly artistic ability, often good at many things including for some having a legal mind because l's intuitive abilities and excellent memory guide them in direct ways. They also operate on a sacred energy that in truth requires time to self and with others, while also being psychically curious through exposure which can lead them towards new age/metaphysical/philosophical studies and activities later in life.

L's also love to sing, they are good speakers and have a great voice that is hard to forget. Self expression being apart of their core, they must be permitted and encouraged to express themselves. Those with more than one L are often prone to accidents and carelessness because so much is on their mind - when things don't go right they act out fears, sorrow, frustration, and profound coldness. Otherwise L's exhibit a happy disposition, are friendly, and sociable if even some may be shy at first meeting. Moreover, L's are avid and quick learners, and many will obtain higher degrees and/or stay in close touch and proximity to and with those in tune with latest trends, knowledge, books, designs, gaming softwares, and philosophies. Learning matters to them - some by merely seeing and others reading, and writing. Life and lifestyle has significant connection even more with the core, family and thus being apart of a solid foundation that enables alignment in their evolving lives. They come with passion of many types, through and with it they come to see and to bring worlds together, long separate that through connection can bring a better future of universal love.

M

Mm

"The Dynamic Mastermind of Multitudes"

Numeric Value: 13   THIRTEEN
Natural Ruling Element: Earth
Planetary Ruling: Sun, Jupiter & Uranus
Vibrational Grouping: The Seekers

Destined Purpose: to master, to survive, to overcome, to strengthen, to empower, to see and therefore to know

Keyword Characteristics: peaks/valleys, tests, lessons, strength, manager, organized, higher ideals

Whenever M is present,

The Opportunities: to activate creativity that opens doorways and crossroads, to express thyself find effective management of self and crossroads, to express thyself and new beginnings, be a model and inspiration, balanced, be the compassion that is a wayshower for others.

The Lessons/Tests: shine smartly, have faith in what may be deemed impossible, to be fearless with intelligence, to have and harness life and emotional balance, to allow creativity to become lifelong legacy.

M's bring great sight and thought upon the home, the family, and the foundation after the open wide world that L engages and vibrationally activates. M's deal with many peaks and valleys on the path sometimes of walking between many worlds, even twice again. Their hearing sight, the facing of self and the inward self amid changes and overturns is unfound in any other letter because the greatest foundation for this vibration is the house of self which they come to do more than see, hear, and merely probe, but through it to emerge greatly transformed. They stand forever next to and in full connection to creativity, charm, wit, and multitudes of gifts and abilities more than others many readily know and while for the deeply attuned in by and through merging into multitudes of thyself, M's confront hardships, panorama sometimes of cycles of deaths around them and even deaths of themselves that brings an unexpected and profound crossroads, propelling an even more transformed master.

Here lies the self, origins, self-starter, pioneer, expert, and boss among the M vibration. The personal bridge and embodiment of heaven and earth. The self and the cosmos become entangled in choices, alignment, standing alone finding strength in the divine self. Things come together for M's in divine experience through a trio, triple vibration, and variation of life experiences, more many and multitudes of beingness which they become masterminds/through the learning most. Past life and past decisions have great bearing on path of M's ears to the past and good memory benefit how they navigate life. Often they stay on the go, ever moving out and onward. There is an endless quest for stability through crossroads that forces them to see, experience, and therefore to know more. Guarding conservative at times, but they also go deep in truth seeking and truth telling and understanding, getting rooted, practicality, security, stability, depth, intensity, and activating sites of knowledge. The builder, designer, concentration of energies formulaic taskmaster therefore they are great on detail, deriving clear understandings of productivity through order, systems, discipline, inner workings, practice and relentless self-discipline.

M's they are among "The Seekers" Learning comes natural and for a great many it's a natural attraction for the high vibrational ever bound to tap the veils of knowledge and deeper understanding. They are ruled by a trio of planetary influences with the Sun, Jupiter, and Uranus revealing not only the charm and how they operate best in the light sometimes even appealing on stage to masses. Their sight, mind, and knowledge runs massively deep with great potential always to not only quickly download and process information, but to electrify others and global many through empowerment and close sharing of universal mysteries and often hidden truths.

They are the letter of creation. They are deeply instinctive about how best to survive, endure, overcome, and to transform. Many dream a lot and can see clarity of truth on the path through such serving as dream interpreters, counselors, teachers, spiritual teachers, life coaches, psychologists and much more. They come to bear a lot and through the life path they expand and reveal even greater strength of character, which also reflects the symbolic waves and motion of water of which many will have to swim to truly learn and master their deeper true self. Ruled by natural elements of Earth, they produce, they experience, they plant seeds, and they serve as a bridge of connectivity between distinct worlds and thus knowing how to appeal to through and with different yet everyday crowds.

Symbolically their path matches their life. They stand well balanced and on two, and even three feet, where victory is theirs over and over again many times, spaces, places, obstacles, and celebrations. They have and are strength of character, facing things head on that others could not survive the crushing weight of. Above all, this vibration is about movement, a wave showing the motion of water; therein standing in a sea of life flow and changes. The v is prominent in the upper middle, facing out to the world, showing their openness to ideas from the higher planes, their arms outstretched suggests calling/opening for spiritual help. M's greatness lies in high or visual impact and openness to the higher realms. They also can be challenged with their eyesight later in life in order to test their full cosmic seeing and activating the inner sight. Moreover M embodies impeccable management abilities. They are often in authoritative roles and many tend to have an orderly mind and excellent memory. This letter is very much about and perhaps all the time about business, pointing to strong managerial abilities always devising new ways on how to activate abundance for self and the family. For some this letter vibration is associated with the quiet of a great sea whose deep waters are mute, shared only when necessary, yet from it life springs forth. M's overall represents change and not endings, but evolutions and contours unexpected that lead to incredible greatness. Among the low vibrational some M's can appear dull, cold, hard, detached, inexpressive or even careless, but more often than not the world gains through M's remarkable charisma, eloquence, balance, wit, well of wisdom, deep love, joy, and magnetic appeal.

N

Nn

"The Ladder of Growth & Universal Expansion"

Numeric Value: 14   FOURTEEN
Natural Ruling Element: Air
Planetary Ruling: Sun, Uranus, and Mercury
Vibrational Grouping: The Seekers

Destined Purpose: to learn, to see , to help, to empower, to transform, to ascend beyond imagination

Keyword Characteristics: bridge, climber, intelligent, growth, navigator, knower, big heart

Whenever N is present,
>*The Opportunities:* to step through the crossroads, and be the change maker, to be fearless, emotionally balanced, to climb and therefore show others new ways to navigate the world.

>*The Lessons/Tests:* to guard against anxieties, to shine with intelligence, to find balance of life emotionally and most especially of the mind.

N's bring ladders of even higher growth after the vibration of self, home, and dynamism of the mind and managing multitudes that letter M ignites. N are however of a different type of expansion and building that is both internal and external. Their path and symbolic makeup has the peaks and valleys of deep obstacles, but with it also comes surrender, tapping into the universal vibration and transformation that lends greater depth of living and understanding after the changes and intensity of life.

N's stand in and forever within an abode of crossroads that forces seeing more. Even for some higher deaths of those close to them that through it moves them into new realms of beingness that facilities even deeper soul changes. Ruled by Air they are communicators, and also open to new experiences, with often far more restraint but in surrendering they learn more about themselves, the worlds around them, and the people included. They are among the cosmic group, "The Seekers," so to learn is to be open to and thus ever seeking out more in the life path. Their mind moves fast and they shine best through empowerment, often thinking fast through electrifying moments. The greatest realm of power for the N vibration lies within their mind and sharing of information and communicating new ideas with a wider world. For they are here to learn, to hear, to share to transform and to be invariably transformed through the process.

N's activate growth above all. Some have heightened sense of smell because this letter connects with humanity and the five senses. This gift arises on the path of those seeking spirit in order to master thoughts and deeper actions. Thoughts for N's are like fish in the great sea of the mind. They are typically very well balanced. Symbolically its inverted V downward open to the material world. While the right V is looking up to something greater: ideas, spiritual understanding, and receptivity to metaphysical unfoldment. Most N's are versatile as are many profound changes in their life - marriage, travel, some may even exhibit psychic awareness, subtleties that may not be used perhaps until later in life or kept hidden from public knowledge. N's many have great imaginations. The symbol of N is used to signify scribe, thus among this vibration are found many good writers with great imaginations and ease of ability to appeal to emotions through written words. N's are tapped into the universe and easily able to download and have success with what to others seems they pick up ideas out of virtually thin air.

O

Oo

"The Divine Mirror of Sight & Evolution"

Numeric Value: 15 FIFTEEN
Natural Ruling Element: Earth
Planetary Ruling: Sun, Mercury, and Venus
Vibrational Grouping: The Inner Doorways

Destined Purpose: to see, to learn, to let go, to find balance, and to be the balance.

Keyword Characteristics: seer, knowledge, cosmic mirror, karmic, unity, connected, unbreakable

Whenever O is present,

The Opportunities: to walk into destiny, to see between worlds, to learn great compassion for self and others, to harness and full use the higher mind of inner sight, and be the way shower for many through one's own life lessons.

The Lessons/Tests: finding and living varied every transforming path, to understand non attachment, change, letting go, to express self, and find heart and mind balance.

O's are the cosmic mirror to a deeper self, moving on and through the cycles and wheels that lead to unprecedented transformation. N's bear vibrations on expansion within wider open worlds whereas O's call forth a deeply internal language with interplay of the cosmos. They endure incredible change and must rely on this divine sight, the symbol of both a wheel, a mirror, and also a single eye seeing between worlds that likewise awakens in pronounced ways. O's shine best in their mind and in their hearts when they give of themselves and experiences and basking in the sun that is them and the glow that comes through them. They are among the vibrational group, "The Inner Doorways" because while they shine and appeal far, they are a tricky vibration, charismatic, but ever on the move so it follows are necessary as promises can be shelved and gone broken while other priorities are managed. They can also require substantial time to themselves so that they can go inward and fully understand the task(s) required of them at hand.

They are walking manifesters who can easily create, produce, and appeal to many. They are seers who have innate knowledge far deeper that comes through cycles of living and seeing and can help with galvanizing the energy of many because O's get/can easily appeal to the average person in a unique way. They are the deep dreamers and deep thinkers who spend immense time in the mind, reading, strategizing, plotting for a greater future but bear in mind they may do so alone and even harness outside ideas they keep secret and protected to themselves until they are guided to trust and share. They are incredible teachers, writers, speakers, and orators who come to show others how to activate their voice in a multitude of realms sometimes even all at once. They deal with sometimes unbearable change that can become destiny with fated events that propels even fame for some. It is when they surrender to their core self that divine lightning can strike.

Overall O's are considered the window of the soul, thus the spiritual eye. They vibrationally stand for the cosmos. No matter how you turn it, it retains its shape. They stand ever next to change and can be destiny and/or to activate karma's wrath of responsibility and past choices. Often O's have fixed opinions, especially if the first letter of the name. They can be moody, hide their feelings well, while also becoming possessive. O represents home, family, and finances, so they attract money easily, but should never really take big gambles on money because living ever on a wheel vibrationally they will move through change and therefore comeback for more changes. O's are also highly protective and responsible, often with a more conservative nature. O is an open closed book. They share widely with the world and they can be known to hold internal secrets, keeping people on a need to know basis in their mind. Lower vibrational O's are overly nervous, smug, self-righteous, worrisome, jealous, suspicious, and even dishonest. All in all, O's as the sole full circle of the letter vibrations, they are and thus embody the essence of magic and universal mysteries of life knowing much, while being keys to the multiverses of truth/higher realms.

P

Pp

"The Activator of Thought & Forward Change"

Numeric Value: 16   SIXTEEN
Natural Ruling Element: Earth
Planetary Ruling: Sun, Venus, and Neptune
Vibrational Grouping: The Higher-Minded Driven

Destined Purpose: to move, to ascend, to find roots, to grow, to know, to activate ideas of high intellect

Keyword Characteristics: smart, higher minded, forward moving, roots, family, higher consciousness

Whenever P is present,
> *The Opportunities:* to honor the sacred self, to use intelligence, to shine and be victorious in life and challenges, to see through illusions, and be balanced in the path.

> *The Lessons/Tests:* intuition, balancing mind of emotions, activating self and magic, walking through incredible obstacles with heart sight and clarity.

P's bring a higher and far greater perspective after the karmic wheel has vibrationally turned through the evolution of experiences with the letter O. As the quintessential awakeners, P's are those still awakening to more and many in the world and of themselves. They are conscientious of self and their body, and later in life spirit and religion/metaphysical interests may take on a greater curiosity, meaning, need, and greater perspective for their growing way forward. P's are ruled by The Sun so they shine through their heart with Venus probing greater abilities to harness the know how moving between illusions and delusions and therefore tapping their own magic and things they love. They are incredible at creativity and production overall, often prevailing far and high above others on the path of productivity. But mostly on their terms most in their own place of solace.

They are electrifying initiators who are a key and in fact hold the mental keys for others to be deeply empowered. Family, knowledge, and roots matter to them. They may hold and harbor secrets that lie only within their mind, but collective empowerment of others is a vital asset of them to the world in a very spectacular way. The mind matters and through it their life they will always find ways to activate, occupy and drive forward with a fueled higher mind. As such, peace and solitude matters to them greatly so that they can see more clearly the tasks necessary, and often the way to proper solutions. Above all else they prefer having clarity of mind, groundedness, and purpose on the path of living and alignment.

Moreover, P's are endowed with deep intuition, dynamic intelligence, keeping counsel as well as being a vault for others even holding secrets to the grave for those they values. They have incredible inner knowingness when fully awakened. P is a circle on the line, the head on the self, and thus it is an intellectual vibration filled with mental curiosity and excellent concentration. Also indicates a bend towards being opinionated and stubborn with things they like/hold dear. P's can be agnostic, very spiritual, and/or atheistic with a completely closed mind. Very important for P's to balance their interests with studies of philosophy in order to use their power for good rather than selfish desire and material gains. P's can be very domineering, having a big head on matters as well as how best to handle them. P's are not always secure of self and therefore without spiritual awareness they can be moody and ill-natured. Rest/reset however is very important physically, mentally, and emotionally especially for them. P's can accomplish anything they set their minds to. Because more than most, P's have incredible vibrational purpose elevating the lives of many.

Qq

"The Unique Blending of Universal Consciousness"

Numeric Value: 17   SEVENTEEN
Natural Ruling Element: Fire
Planetary Ruling: Sun, Neptune, Mars
Vibrational Grouping: The Inner Doorways

<u>**Destined Purpose**</u>: to know, to learn, to take the altered path, to use your knowledge

<u>**Keyword Characteristics:**</u> unique, divine consciousness, alignment, expansion, psychic

Whenever Q is present,

The Opportunities: to walk the unique and creative path of production, to see through illusions, have drive and heart, to see beyond others and to spark the truth of self.

The Lessons/Tests: to survive life changes and transformations, to have balance in self and self expression, to see all sides and perspectives, and to be fearless in/on the unique path forward.

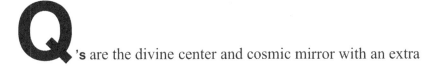

Q's are the divine center and cosmic mirror with an extra hook. They are more than any other letter profoundly parallel to the letter O, however the line flowing out towards a point is a/the divine rod and extension of immense power that only Q wearers can choose to activate the where, when, or how. They are ruled by a trio threat of planetary influences indicating that they shine best in and within groups, doing so they illuminate far and wide, and in unexpected ways albeit at times driven by oddities, illusions or continuously activating magic unseen and all around them. They are of a higher vibration symbolic of themselves they are God's universes mouthpiece where they are tuned in and divinely wired in a way that lends incredible psychic awareness. They just know they are on a very deep level living both conscious and unconscious.

Q's being numeric value of 17 says they are the awakened, awakening, and that they stand next to alignment this merging of self through the blending of the highest self will enable enormous power and through it abundance, multidimensionality, and unlimited potential for fame emerges. If, when, and how they choose to activate their God center within their mind. They come to know, to be, and to experience fire on the path. They are also here to be the extension of the self as an embodiment and emboldened ray bringing universal consciousness that is strengthened through hardship, surrender, and having compassion in and of the world. Qs can keep secrets tucked away that create peculiar behavior unless they use their sufferings as stories of triumph and the empowerment of others. They learn from life lessons and sometimes have to redo things until they decide to move off the karmic path and wheel of tribulations. Moreover, Q's are of a universally special vibration can choose the higher path of connection or plunge into the lower vibrational rungs and criminal elements. Lower vibrational can be deeply negative and often dangerous in worldly dealings with others because of their power that runs deep. The choice is always theirs. It is however about walking the path to greatest happiness, no matter how divinely unique,

Q's are fundamentally about balancing physical and mental forces, as Q's are active on both planes. Q's do not like being alone. Most times Q's are willing to give of themselves almost 100 percent of the time. They also seem to have a knack for making money, and truly want the best that they can have. Within them you see much originality often quite psychic and deep learners open to knowledge and communication. They are here to balance energies in light of spiritual knowledge. Q's are an initiation which comes through many trials, tests, and significant losses. For them the secret solution is balance will always be. The circle represents the spiritual sun, the line is the rod of balance, alluding to the head and the tongue demonstrating why some become speakers, communicators, counselors, channelers, caregivers, and humanitarians for the world.

R

Rr

"The Spark of Creativity & Transformational Fire"

Numeric Value: 18   EIGHTEEN
Natural Ruling Element: Fire
Planetary Ruling: The Sun/Mars/Neptune
Vibrational Grouping: The Higher-Minded Driven

Destined Purpose: to test, to be tested, to learn, to experience rebirth/regrowth, to rise above, to see in all its realms.

Keyword Characteristics: efficiency, self determination, compassion, practical intelligence, and magnetic charm.

Whenever R is present,

The Opportunities: to stand in your dimensional power, to let go of old ways, activate abundance, to create a legacy far beyond the present path.

The Lessons/Tests: to balance the drive forward, to move past illusions of self, to let go of secrets and parts of the past, and to balance the susceptible influence of lower vibrations.

R's bring the strongest vibration of real life. While Q's bring the rather unique, R's always carry the real, raw, rhythmic, relentlessness, even rage. They are many things and above all, direct honest and full of intense fire that can open many doors to new beginnings and even burn bridges that they may later regret when operating on impulse. They being incredible at the know how on selling, change, explosive power, entanglements, emotions, traps, webs, dimensions, and the need for activation of the higher mind when fueled on a higher vibration.

R's are intentional, impactful and dynamic with intelligence especially with how far they will go in the plunge for truth and or to hide deep dark secrets for much of their life. They are practical and they shine with others best in showing by helping the empowerment on the drive forward. Because they are ruled by The Sun they are enlightenment and they enlighten by loving, not just average living, with the fire raging within as their natural ruling element they are able to draw upon the flame more than most to see through illusions and traps of loyalty to breathe and walk through transformed with magic and activation at their cellular core ever in full operation

They are wizards in many kinds and therefore greatly influential on the masses - some high, some low but aspects of them are remembered by those aware and or mindful. They come to learn how to be and how to harness the dragon. Symbolically they vibrationally parallel both letter P and letter K, the primary difference being that unlike P, they have a hind leg, an anchor, line of Gods center flowing out, open mouth flowing and tongue wagging. They are divinely creative able to produce in a wide range of making many things, creating music, singing, drawing, painting, talents unseen with immense rarity and future global curiosity.

Numerically, they are number 18 which points to a critical thematic triage ever flowing in their life about the self, ego, emotions, power, secrets, ambition, drive, higher mind, letting go of attachments, and having unconditional love. They come to find their power but also to let go. Through it they teach us and the wider world rears them and especially on the spectrum of rebirthing towards creating an even better self anew and transform through many profound moments, lives, and what may seem fractured futures bringing change and the reborn. The bigger key for R is when, where, and how they activate the many sparks of intelligent creative and fire they manifest through their presence and being. They inspire

82

confidence in people like no others and they tend to give without a thought of return and even for the joy of it. In the same vein however R's can be rugged, mean, cruel, and downright authoritative and nasty in their dealings with others, especially those they detest, look down upon, and/or want nothing further to do with. They are intense, driven, and undeniably passionate in the feelings and view of the world.

Symbolically R begins with a vertical line on the left representing an upright person. The loop at the top is the head and stands for the ability to think, to draw in knowledge, to have profound creative thought. There is much power that R's can use for either constructive or destructive purposes. Within R's there are many criminals and many celebrities of global appeal. However R evolves depends greatly on their upbringing. It is only until the bearer outgrows self seeking interests, gains emotional maturity, and seeks higher levels of expression that life will manifests, tilting towards who they emotionally and psychically are. with a series of difficulties. R's are intellectuals given the ability of retaining knowledge and thinking deeply on things. Even more, R's are the most understanding given the inclination deep desire for unity and the spirit of brotherhood/sisterhood.

S

Ss

"The Transformer of Soul Wisdom & Ancient Memory"

Numeric Value: 19   NINETEEN
Natural Ruling Element: Fire
Planetary Ruling: Sun/Neptune/Saturn
Vibrational Grouping: The Multipronged Transformers

Destined Purpose: to see, to learn, to empower a great many, to remember and overcome, to transform, and to achieve high intelligence for self and the world.

Keyword Characteristics: wisdom, moving between worlds, t transformation, igniter, supreme intellect, and fire.

Whenever S is present,

The Opportunities: to see self on an large stage, honor playfulness, to be a higher vibrational bridge for others, to see multiple perspectives, be open to change, and forge legacies by creating knowledge.

The Lessons/Tests: letting go, experiencing changes and attending lessons, to remain forward moving amid obstacles and hardships, to learn alignment, balance, and value of self and innate knowledge.

S's move in multiple directions - at once seeing the future, remembering the past, and transforming through with and on it that extends the mind and soul being back out from roots, material, grounded living of mid world that R is grounded with fired intensity. S is fire but in a truly higher minded way. They are symbolic of kundalini and the serpent rising to wisdom, the seer who must endure immediate and abrupt changes the one whose path will be different from the beginning while the past life is deeply influential in a myriad of dynamic ways unseen.

S's are intellectual, they are depth, movement, travel, empowerment and the lifelong student, and intellect. They are highly driven. With the Sun, as one of 3 planets shines upon on their path, penetrating depth of illumination and the getting of vital information. They have the innate ability to tap and reveal often centuries-old knowledge and oracle like messages. They come to gain, to give, and to be transformed in body, mind, and soul. With Neptune and Saturn similarly ruling their cycle from the planetary realms in massive ways they come to le/relearn their magic, being cautionary of other's illusions and unexpected delusions that can hinder and therefore blind the magical pathway forward. As seers, S's are deeply psychic, able to see and understand and many times walk between multiple worlds with magnetism, wit, and charm that electrifies an exceptionally large global mass. What they think, write, know is the fire of deep wisdom that pours on to them quickly and forcefully from the many higher realms.

Ruled by number 19, they stand next to expansion and tending to the higher mind and higher knowledge. They also come to find balance and learn peace of the entire being. For fires of ambition, drive, entrepreneurial forward spirit, movement burrows deep within many S's. They are master transformers and tapped far deeply in on ancient memory of who and what once was and shall be. They are the embodied memories of one, sum, and multidimensional all of highest vibration, realm connection as well as access. They can walk worlds, some are abundantly successful in the material world while can spiritwalk and connect with higher dimensions, spirit animals, as well as crack codes that may not be fully understood for many future lives of others. Among some S's bearing old souls, they come to ensure an enlightened future more than the present can and will ever imagine. The divergence S vibration is anchored on changes, itches of new beginnings, staying forever on the move, and the ever quest for a new depth of truth and activation of once hidden knowledge.

S's are considered the mother letter of creation and represent the element of fire. They experience many choices and decisions on the path that activates realms of inner consciousness while connecting realms of often extrasensory awareness. This vibration is the way of truth and life. Some often barely finishes one project when ready to start another, thus self starters and achiever. S's are very creative and they set sights high although assumed to be striving for perfection, but really for them it is about the acquisition of a depth of knowledge that leads to greatest success. They are very ambitious and most times have a relentless drive forward. They also tend to enjoy working alone, and do their best without interference. S as a health factor they must guard against fatigue, over exertion, neglected boundaries, overwhelmed feelings, anxiety, depression through massive changes and especially deaths and losses.

Expressing their individuality and worrying less about what others think will fuel them further on the lifepath. They greatly dislike taking orders because in their mind they know intuitively what they are doing and the best. Some S's can be dramatic and emotional while highly intuitive, being receptive on the spiritual plane. Each C like open moon shining at the top an bottom of S is symbolic of reflecting its light, open to spiritual and mental plane. They not only see both realms and are psychic seeing through the veils of disillusion and hidden truths, but they can also control both worlds. S vibrations undeniably represent the serpent which is of infinite wisdom.

Among the S's here lies consciousness and higher dimensions senses. Upper half faces the future and widely open to spiritual insights, multi talents, intuition, and ideas of creativity come vast and easy. Being open on the spiritual plane many S's enjoy dwelling in the mind. Bottom half symbolically is about the material world, facing it they can remember back to a younger age than most with piercing memory. They may change direction midstream in search for the best approach to a problem. Negative S's are steeped in ego where they speak and think of themselves too much. Without a doubt however all S' assert independence sometimes to their own detriment. Some turn from light to a baser path. S's are ever seeking wisdom for the rising serpent. S is a letter of endurance. The ancients called it the letter of surrender. They can be spiritually intense and can either and/or sting and charm. S's bring higher love and new starts in life and attraction of abundance and money, but their life is far more challenging given the contours of changes that directly alter the path and disrupt what may seem familiar. S's at peak will triumph over obstacles to attain incredible ambitions. There will be many turnings in the life path along with emotional upheavals, failures, and uncontrolled impulses - all to learn most. Positivity is the key factor environment for them.

T

Tt

"The Genius of Debate, Truth, & Higher Perspective"

Numeric Value: 20   TWENTY
Natural Ruling Element: Earth
Planetary Ruling: The Moon/Venus
Vibrational Grouping: The Higher-Minded Driven

Destined Purpose: to see, to learn, to choose, to find balance with others, to know thyself, to let go of fears, and to be a wayshower.

Keyword Characteristics: higher mind, debate, many perspectives, roots, family, very much in and of the mind, picky, high intellect

Whenever T is present,
> *The Opportunities:* to exhibit mental brilliance, to find balance in the heart, mind, and well of emotions, to empower others, to find roots and deep connection.

> *The Lessons/Tests:* having compassion, being smart with debate; honoring intuition, loving and with proper balance to prevent catastrophic imbalance.

T's are very open, they hear, see, and know quite more than others are fully aware. From the vibration of the ever moving S letter vibration, T's walk a slower path and they have a different focus on roots, core, finding deeper core of alignment that in turn comes with greater depth and a plunge for depth of truth and connection. Ruled by The Moon and Venus, they give with an open heart to those they love and hold close everyone they value. However know too they do not bring everyone close, some T's can be down right cranky, off-putting, uninterested, cool/afloof, unforgiving, and intolerant of some and quite a many. They are like the old wise man of the letters. They have been here often and will ensure you know the extent of their knowledge while often seeing the higher perspective and attempting to maintain peace or instead activating war with it. Without a doubt, they have a propensity for explosive emotions and/or being emotionally withdrawn. Their ears are wide open and memory even more impeccable. Some can be creative, producing at exponentially high rates in short amounts of time, but it will be sometimes dry, on their terms, perhaps uninteresting to some but without a doubt, it will forge legacies that some want to follow.

As the numeric value of 20, these are the geniuses of the vibrational spectrum with exceptionally bright minds along with a veil of emotions that can emerge internal with overthinking, worrying, and stressing about all the details and or be careless and irresponsible laced with combustible emotions shown to the world. No matter the vibrational makeup combined with other letters, T's have come especially to see between worlds, to see into cosmic mirror of the present and many perspectives and even past treatment of others, responsibilities and/or past life learnings.

T's they complete the vibrational evolution garnering wisdom from all that is learned. Symbolically T has a bar that is the roof of the letter representing protection and higher mind. This letter also about hearing. When we listen with inner, we hear, and gain profound wisdom. This letter is truly anchored on a definite spiritual relationship. T equals creation, once horizontal line matter and vertical is spirit descending into matter. They are also about giving selfless service to others, desires partnership in business and marriage, and must learn to give and take. T's reflect self sacrifice throughout the path. Often many have difficult time making decisions because of seeing both sides of a question. Some have deep interest in religion/spirituality while others can be high strung, tense, get carried away with negative emotion, use sarcasm, and even cruel words. More often than not this letter is very much the peacemaker. Two t's in a name can mean getting all bottled up, double cross or tied up situations. Moreover on the lifepath and especially interpersonal connection, to be a good partner T's must be honest and true to self in all their relationships.

U

Uu

"The Empathic Receptor Of & For the World"

Numeric Value: 21   TWENTY ONE
Natural Ruling Element: Water
Planetary Ruling: The Moon/The Sun
Vibrational Grouping: The Universal Surrenderers

Destined Purpose: to feel, to express, to see and to live balance and activate emotional intelligence and harness emotional harmony with others.

Keyword Characteristics: emotions, cups of knowledge and memory, water, truth, and depth

Whenever U is present,
> *The Opportunities:* to learn self in and with the world, to honor their emotions, to find deep balance in life, to trust/activate intuitions, to be the wayshower of much.

> *The Lessons/Tests:* experience multiple obstacles and overcoming through the lesson; to manage life and self, to shine in wisdom, to experience self in best way for the path.

U's bring emotions, inspiration, and good fortune. If T can get wound and tied up most often in their mind, then U's offer an immersion into an unprecedented veil of high emotions, empathy, and insight in a pronounced unique way. They are very open to the world, the universe, and multiverses making them an incredible receptor of insight and higher information as well as being deeply empathic, where they feel others. Feeling is an incredible vibration and U's are the creative imagine charming with openness to receive many talents and give immensely to the world. Ruled by the Moon further amplifies their emotions, empathic antenna, intuition, and overall psychic awareness. The Sun allows them to shine in the world and most especially when they know themselves, meaning they are therefore in tune with the uniqueness of divine gifts, feelings, and pronounced knowingness. Interestingly, with the natural element of Water apart of their cosmic vibration, this points to seeing between worlds, harnessing greater survival and being ever-present spark of astute creativity.

U's more than most, they come to feel and to make others feel it; for it is their core symbology. They appear half parallel with Q however far less closed off, U's feel immensely giving far greater knowingness. They also are way more open to the universe, the teachings, the gifts, the downloads, therefore, they at times may need far more time from the world and all its ever-shifting interplay of vibrations that extends out often unknowing to many. Without a doubt, balance in and with meditation, music rechanneling their energy toward higher vibrations can help fuel the passion, the depth of emotional feeling because over time they will require far more emotional intelligence in the where and how to allow the flow of the full self and when to have and show restraint as well as implement boundaries.

As vibrational sponges in many senses of the absorbable cosmos, U's come to find to show to exact and to transform self. However they come most to do so through choices in and of the world and other people. Aspects of their life they may find overdoing it an ongoing theme they have to balance and moreover alter in the right way to better fuel their best creativity and full energy of the whole self. Yet putting self and others needs 1st while giving in the universal ways of compassion, it must find the way back to you that allows a transformed self to rise and therefore give even more. Perhaps later in the adult years that activates vibrationally layered self with many more rays to extend to the world with the multi-talents. One should never assume basic and averageness with U's ever, they are unable to hide their feelings being too open as a amplified rod of many dynamics. Even more, they are exceptionally unique in so on the path being of numeric value 21 shows, even more, the brilliance and high intellect and emotions that can ignite incredible even unusual art, music, and beauty and writing - moreover something that shows the cup of direct knowledge and higher sourced vibration they are tapped into and extend out when and only they choose to. The low vibrational withhold talents of high mastery for reasons and attachments only they know. U's are very much givers in this world so they must be allowed to give and be led likewise to balance most.

Many U's are often good speakers who know very well how to project their voices. Some also have musical abilities and good singing voices. Many U's given an array talents should prepare for the future if merely because they can tend to take on too much and may hold onto things for too long as they are also enthusiastic collectors. Very good with words, they can be either very articulate or they may remain silent and uncommunicative. Some in fact many U's can be overly sensitive. The straight lines in the letter indicate two emotional outlets, thus a dual nature: many can be faddish and liberal or possess high ideals and act out more conservative ideals. U's overall can be either warm and spiritual or cold and materialistic. They are however more open to universal consciousness than most. Negatives are that they can bring jealous, temperamental, quarrelsome, often be deeply indecisive and sarcastic. U's they can and will rock and spill out contents like a cup and easily so if not carefully managed. If U's fill their cup through selfishness and greed. they sometimes hold a lot inside where some can become overly nervous or emotional leading to nervous tension, headaches and/or challenges in maintaining their equilibrium. Balance for this vibration of all is pertinent to the dynamism U's are not only capable of vibrationally emitting, but offering in an unexpected and immensely profound way to the world.

V

Vv
"The Ignitor of Universal Knowledge & Intuitive Victories"

Numeric Value: 22   TWENTY TWO
Natural Ruling Element: Air
Planetary Ruling: Double Vibration of The Moon
Vibrational Grouping: The Universal Surrenderers

Destined Purpose: to feel, to show, to surrender, to learn, to have faith, to achieve, and to find joy on the lifepath

Keyword Characteristics: victorious, supreme intellect, peaks, valleys, resiliency, emotional and psychic intelligence.

Whenever V is present,

The Opportunities: to be a master builder of knowledge/progress, to change the world, to have faith in self and ideas, to activate the mind and emotions in profound ways.

The Lessons/Tests: to endure, survive, and to rise above low points, to shine in and with good intentions; to manage life peaks valleys, let go; go with the flow know all that is divine.

V's are deep vortexes of higher knowledge. After the emotions of U comes V the sharper edges of brilliance often a genius mind that has enormous influence close and even more afar. U's are V's and V's symbolically match U's however V's have sharper edges thus valleys and deeper plunges that bring high emotions, an intense depth of the mind, incredible resilience and victories unseen in many letter vibrations. They are truly high-level masters, they feel everything, and despite others disbelief at times the massive amount of information that takes in processes, memorizes, and can compile for the far bigger picture of understanding is truly unparalleled. Evidenced most by their being numeric value of 22, thus double high vibration of the mind, the emotions, and of the truly master builder. They will care about the family, learning, being their true free self, and the long term legacy of the future to ensure it extends beyond their living. They are supreme masters of information as well as feeling knowledge that carries deeply acute intuitive psychic abilities: dreams, clairvoyance, telepathy, and much more that age and maturity will appear as others untapped gifts reveal themselves. V's come to give, to endure, to rise up, and to be victorious in a multitude of ways. Change will deeply and unexpectedly prevail around them and for some emotions can and will cloud mature judgment, they eventually come full circle- after the lessons that emerge through with the peaks and valleys. They are super sensitive in an emotional way that can hold resentment and hurt feelings for longer periods until they are fully ready to let go, release, and overcome. But the sharpness of their lines, unending yet perhaps an L turned diagonally, indicates that the lessons of love come with intensity, jaw-dropping changes and surrender to the higher realms of divinity on and how on the lifepath continues and contours. Much of this attests to the ever ruling element of "Air" within which they can share far and wide transforming many but they are fundamentally open, lending access to new and innovative yet practical information they will gladly share.

Moreover, with the double vibration of the Moon, stronger than any letter vibration, V's bear the mark of truly profound intuition. Some may intentionally overlook such gifts of sight and therefore withhold sharing the extent to perhaps seeing through the veil to the undead/still living, while likewise leaving unrevealed the how of their seemingly natural psychic ability. Their vibration is unique and highly developed frequency unmatched most times with peers and family ever sometimes. They can prevail over seemingly the impossible with multiple victories along the way unattainable and unreachable for some, but they also can have hard lessons in sharp contrast to others. It is all apart of the universal divine plan of evolutionary experiences through vibrations on the winding lifepath.

V's are completely open to the universal understandings, very intellectual, and typically have a good business head. Many can and will work very well with others. They may gravitate and find enjoyment in studying metaphysics given their capacity for higher intellect. As a V letter they have no line separating the spiritual realm the material plane. Those who are materialistc leanings can be unscrupulous business people and in some cases even hardened criminals. All V's they need good to be able to contribute something of worth to be fulfilled. Some tend to have nervous energy and the inverted v is a mountain peak. Interestingly, many often feel they have to climb mountains to achieve what they desire. They will spend all their money on their desires and then feel a need for financial security. Insecure desires are high many among the V vibration, and therefore it is important for them to have deeper understanding of self and future, finances especially. They need spiritual enlightenment to balance the nervousness and bring desired inner peace. V is always looking lifted to the universe in asking for spiritual help or vibrational understandings. They are without a doubt very open and interestingly in tune with to new age metaphysical, kemetic studies, practices, and activities as they are entirely open to receive ideas and to build upon and manifest larger projects and visions. They have immeasurable strength and will work hard, for they are without a doubt the truly the number of the tireless worker. V's love their family very much and will work hard to provide for them in every way. For them part of their lesson is recognizing that all life is a sacred gift including to receive as well as give. In perhaps magical ways V's overall are easily able to manifest, especially for ideas to work for them better than anyone since they have natural channeling abilities that actualize projects and entrepreneurial goals and dreams. Given that they are able to set new goals and achieve them again and again. For they are among the ever victorious!

Ww

"The Manifester of Inner Wisdom & Freedom"

Numeric Value: 23   TWENTY THREE
Natural Ruling Element: Air
Planetary Ruling: The Moon/Jupiter
Vibrational Grouping: The Universal Surrenderers

Destined Purpose: to surrender, to live a high vibrational life, to learn, to let go, to empower, and most to find balance

Keyword Characteristics: depth of knowledge, wise, surrender, multitudes, wheels turning

Whenever W is present,
> *The Opportunities:* to surrender and find faith in self and the lifepath, to experience change with profound resilience, to share knowledge, to dream big

> *The Lessons/Tests:* to let go, to see value in self and others lifepath, to see and walk between many worlds, to be and see the blessing on the lifepath.

W's are a double high vibration of surrender, the mind of emotions, creative expression, and waves of deep changes in and all around them. Symbolically W's, in essence, are V's interlinked in the uplift and empowerment and higher movement of self and others in and through peaks and valleys, overcoming and even reliving an entire new path and parallel life. Without a doubt, W's know about and are incredible manifesters. Some are telepathic while others fearlessly vocalize in charming ways towards getting the job done. Their path and complete vibrational bandwidth is significantly high which it brings knowledge, street smarts, wit, and a pendulum of life living and transforming.

W's are ruled by The Moon and Jupiter, its big, its intuitive, and without a doubt emotions will be revealed and or erupt in massive form through passion, drive, knowingness of the way forward, and even the astute way forward to change. They live and are the Air embodying its meaning where change and restlessness and travel given deep desires for movement apart of the vibrational pattern of being and learning for them. They have unique inner wisdom that they are not afraid of showing and activating, ever. The wheels for them must always move forward turning toward something. As high vibrations, they are very active, strong, and responsive. Emotions and the past can spill over for them where karma can take unique and unexpected form permitting deeper and even long term influential learning.

Moreover W's signify the eye of humans that sees light and the ear that hears the sound of air and wind. With a deeper sensitivity, making it a much more emotional vibration. they have a need for freedom in order to cope with constant changes that can emerge within their lives. They can often overindulge in sensual pleasures, or expressiving negative traits that is when living in the valleys or pits of the W. The peaks for a w's life can be very high and in some cultures this letter speak towards a "limited Master" wise men able to transcend and master themselves to delve into greater spirituality. They are regarded as the likeness of deepest mystery because of the two deep valleys the letter stands on. Often w's have a change in consciousness at some time in their lives. It is through these peaks that their arms are seeking greater enlightenment and inspiration. They are capable of the rare inner voice and accessing the subtlties of the universe.

Xx

"The Crossroads of Multi-Conversations"

Numeric Value: 24   TWENTY-FOUR
Natural Ruling Element: Water
Planetary Ruling: The Moon, Uranus, and Venus
Vibrational Grouping: The Universal Surrenderers

<u>**Destined Purpose**</u>: to feel, to show, to know, to give, to move forward on the right path.

<u>**Keyword Characteristics**</u>: crossroads, conversation, open, emotions, psychic, expressive

Whenever X is present,

The Opportunities: to use your intellect, to hear, see, feel, know, and walk into destiny; to connect to and for many, to be unafraid to show emotions.

The Lessons/Tests: to expect the unexpected, to remain forward moving, to love and find proper heart sight and heart balance on the lifepath.

X's mark the spot in a fascinating way because they are and embody destiny. Their minds are wired in such a way for some to see through past the wheel beyond the crossroads of living and even becoming the way-shower for others. Every core being and the full makeup of X's is open in every single direction. They are the only letter equally open on all sides. This points to extremely high sensory empathic abilities that for some can either be overbearing until properly channeled and/or perhaps disregarded or even being unfelt, if their path requires a different type of vibrational living - autism, blindness, deaf - that feels disconnected until a transformation on the life path that alters them and psychic physical knowingness.

Ruled by The Moon they show deep emotions, substantial compassion even for the world and others. With both Uranus and Venus apart of their vibrational makeup by planetary influence, they are super responsive, confronting the massive unexpected that can activate and alter the heart of how to live with and through the heart. The ruling element of water further triples the emotions, the intuition, and the need for surrender. Many times X are very chatty, high energy and some even have nervous energy making them hyper and or excited all the time. They are also often super intelligent in ways deeply innate, while the need for roots, stability and family matters to them where some have to either learn to come uncoiled/share more with the world and find proper balance of their body, mind, and spirit in a truly unique way. X's come to feel and to show us all the worldly meaning of receptivity, being another type of vibrational reflection and open channel of and moreover how we manage such universal gifts. They come psychically attuned in ways maybe perceived odd by some and extraordinary by others. Additionally, expression is most to be and to show the now for many including the near and far future.

Moreover all X's represent wisdom, magnetic personality, they are very much about love and family. X's can also exe itself out, if it feels another has crossed it, can become bitter, seek revenge, and self denial. X's very much stand strong on the earth plane and thus remain open to materialism; arms outstretched asking for spiritual help. Therefore x's can be all spiritual all material, high-minded or abused and fearful. They tend to have falls and accidents unless the person taps their spiritual universal consciousness. X's are very open and receptive to psychic powers but some may rarely use. They feel things deeply, and its sorrows can be truly intense. Its desire to improve conditions of humanity or family/friends that can be so intense that some will sacrifice to do so. The v's on all sides of letter X symbolically indicates a bit of nervous energy and supersensitivity and empathic connections. X marks the spot implies moreover they are universally connected with universal consciousness and even for some the idea of a cross or Christ principle. They being the vibration fully giving of self to the world and in turn receiving.

Y

Yy
"The Divine Rod of Truth & Choices"

Numeric Value: 25   TWENTY FIVE
Natural Ruling Element: Earth
Planetary Ruling: The Moon, Mercury, and Neptune
Vibrational Grouping: The Universal Surrenderers

Destined Purpose: to see, to know truth, to have faith in self/choices, to find mental and emotional balance, and to emit harmony in and outward.

Keyword Characteristics: truth, choice, movement, open, road/way, rod, channeling.

Whenever Y is present,
> *The Opportunities:* to live in truth, to be clear on the path of choices, to use intellect, to find balance within the mind, emotions and rivers of change.

> *The Lessons/Tests:* to guard against uncertainties, to believe in self and your abilities, to let go and have faith in the future, to use the higher mind and to rise above illusions of self and others.

Y's bring the core back from the wide open world to choice, truth, and establishing the foundation of self and vibrational living. Y's are indeed a divine lightning rod. Through it the vibration brings enormous choice and enormous truth. For they are some of the greatest awakeners who came to empower others, endure choice and change, and to have faith on the lifepath. They are intuitive, kind, compassionate, deeply mental, and either they weigh on the side of illusions or they are more tapped in on their magical side which will carry them far in their dealings with everyday others. The trio planetary ruling of The Moon, Mercury, Neptune within their vibration thus ensures a smart mind, emotional intelligence, and deep knowingness on how best to navigate the sea of future opportunities and choices on the future that can and will arise.

Symbolically they are aspects of an I, U, and semi-inverted J, all which points to emotions, hearing between and through more. Having an incredible mind, memory, knowingness with pronounced intellect such intelligence of varying kind for them can cause the need for greater alone time to delve deep into their studies - metaphysical, complex philosophies and technologies. Moreover, they are a sacred vibration with sometimes sharp angles not readily understood by others but where an incredible well of talents can overflow. So long as they stay or get rooted and therefore grounded on the life path will bring change most through forward movement, joy, freedom, and being their true self.

Ruled by the Earth allows greater potential for creativity, therein the broad path of materiality is seen as earth wisdom that comes with trial and error or right hand the path of divine wisdom, universal consciousness, godliness and virtues seeing them through closer narrow gaze required with choices at the forking of the ways. Many Y's have a deep desire to learn the mystical and mysteries of life. They are shaped like a divining rod, that draws the person deeper to the study of esoteric, spiritual, cosmic consciousness. There may be psychic experiences and or a true search for wisdom for some. Without a doubt they are bound to spiritual unfoldment on the path because of the drawing power to deeper inward reflection. They are often deep thinkers, idle talk can be discomforting. For some as they think through much. Those with materialist leaning have urgings to study even deeper as they go far in the plunge. Some can be loners and prone to excess sensual temptations. There will be decisions that will have to be made quickly and that may prove difficult for Y's, their path always is about clarity, truth, and the right choice. They must therefore learn to hear and trust the inner voice guiding forward and through it decisions will get easier. Y points out the path to god. Sometimes there can be a desire for quiet, rest, and most of all peaceful surroundings.

Z

Zz
"The Psychic Seer of Deep Emotions"

Numeric Value: 26   TWENTY SIX
Natural Ruling Element: Water
Planetary Ruling: The Moon/Venus/Mars
Vibrational Grouping: The Seers

Destined Purpose: to feel, to see, to experience, to decipher, to find balance, to activate core happiness that reflects self and deeper truths.

Keyword Characteristics: seer, seeing, emotionally expressive, deeply loving, psychic, movement in multiple directions, changes, sight, and great many multitudes.

Whenever Z is present,

The Opportunities: to see and find real power latent within self, to walk into destiny with consciousness of abilities, bridge of the mind, body, and emotions.

The Lessons/Tests: to let go, to be ok with self-expression and emotions, to love balanced, be fearless and to be decisive in the forward pathway

Z's are the last and yet incredibly powerful vibration of deep wisdom, psychic abilities, high emotions, and activating real power. Z's are among the greatest of "The Seers" as they have knowingness for them comes if, when and through dreams, chance meetings, at birth, and even higher at the points of so called spirits/ghosts of loved ones in veiled form. They more than others can literally see between worlds the past present and future to the core of living and so called dead.

The cosmic makeup for Z's only enhances all these unique talents, emotions, and intuitive understandings and knowledge base quite profoundly. They are many times fearless or seemingly profess greater courage than may really be at play. Even more, they love hard wide and deep. Unlike many, they can't fake love if merely because they show it, live it profusely. Their symbolism comes with sensitivity that feels more in multiple unexpected directions. Thus why tend to see high anxiety and depression among Z's unable to manage the outpour of emotions fueling from things and moments in the past and present and/or what Z's may feel coming. Ruled by the numeric value of 26 they come to understand the evolutionary meaning of the mind, emotions, consciousness of self, the body, universal spirit, and exacting their power through lessons gained. Above all, they come to walk the dimensions and experience realms of power with/of the self through empowerment and manifestation by ever sharing with others and a great many in their life.; especially through music, art, photography, writing, even multiple births, therein giving their heart to the world. Moreover, with water as their natural elemental ruling core, they see know and they feel quite intensely. Their intuition is superpower and through it they embody psychic seers of deep emotions. In feeling Z's know the world at large learning at immeasurably steep levels.

Their governing influence overall is about movement, they rarely sit still being in the vibration that can be triggered by a lot and or interested in alot. They can be highly analytical and investigate things because they have the innate ability to discover hidden purposes. It is for this reason that Z is interested in and can get to the bottom of undecipherable mysteries and cosmic codes. Z resembles lightning vibration moving in both directions forward browed in the mind, are bottom ever on the move which speaks towards vital equal energy with this letter. This can be used for good or evil to make vibration dthing run smoothly or to destroy. The middle vertical line goes straight from the physical to the spiritual a direct line that which is equal to supplying energy, ideas, and inspiration. Z has acute insight to the spiritual world and can serve as an able leader able to inspire others especially spiritually and through building of new institutions of thought and practice. History has very much shown that Z lettered people and those with Z in their name walk between worlds empowering the past present and future. They on the awakening path, analyze everything, through it mental strains can drain their energy or lead to mental breakdowns that can be overturned by sufficient rest, meditation, and balance that can assist with equilibrium. Often they need more rest than normal letter vibration. Z's are about responsibility and for some that can come with relentless tests on what they need, and even put off that highlights irresponsibilities or achievement. Z's overall are a truly fun, dramatic, and deep vibration many often want around.

Names, Birthdays & The Symbology of Birthtimes

Your name and birthday are two of the most critical components to unlocking your soul contract and learning cosmically who you are, how you are vibrationally wired, and how to tap the the realm of your destined path/purpose(s) as well as your birth time. Decoding core elements of your personal self (the letters and the numbers) you can deepen your awareness of your full cosmic self. Below you are provided with basic decoded breakdowns regarding your name, birthday, and birthtime to empower you on the meanings for the lifepath of self and others. This life, you, and we all have chosen is comprised of vibrational matrix of your name, birthday, and birthtime. To know is to be informed.

Name
First (grounded/strongest identity point/vibrational lead)

Middle (central anchor/vibrational life backdrop)

Last (bridgepoint of expression, vibration inherited/shared vibration)

Birthday
Month (The vibration ((number/letters of the month)) through which we come to learn how to manage, create foundation for our self, and to see, to be the ladder and bridge through core learning)

Day (The doorway vibration to our deeper core self that shows a new self and options endlessly on the path that we come to learn)

Year (The pathway to choice and truth shared by things/born that year)

Birthtime
AM Born (the vibration of activation, energy, anxiety, and duality)

PM Born (the vibration of roots, highermind, forwardness & karma)

Recommended Readings

1. Shirley Lawrence, *The Secret Science of Numerology: The Hidden Meaning of Numbers and Letters* (Page Books, 2011)
2. Alison Baughman, *Speaking to Your Soul: Through Numerology* (Createspace, 2013).
3. The Cosmic Doc, *Numerology 101: Everyday Numbers, Decode the Vibration*, (CreateSpace, 2018)
4. Matthew Oliver Goodwin, *Numerology, The Complete Book* (New Page Books 2005).
5. Faith Javane and Dusty Bunker, *Numerology & The Divine Triangle,* (ParaResearch, 1979).
6. Lloyd Stratton, *Numbers and You: A Numerology Guide for Everyday Living* (Ballantine Books, 1987).